Plan & Go | Kungsleden

All you need to know to complete Sweden's Royal Trail

Danielle Fenton, Wayne Fenton

sandiburg press

Plan & Go | Kungsleden

All you need to know to complete Sweden's Royal Trail

Published by sandiburg press
www.sandiburgpress.com

Cover photos: Alisvággi Valley (front); En Route to Serve STF Hut (back)

SAFETY NOTICE: This book describes physically challenging activities in remote outdoor environments which carry an inherent risk of personal injury or death. While the author(s) and sandiburg press have made every effort to ensure that the information contained herein was accurate at the time of publication, they are not liable for any damage, injury, loss, or inconvenience arising directly or indirectly from using this book. Your safety and health during preparations and on the trail are your responsibility. This book does not imply that any of the trails described herein are appropriate for you. Make sure you fully understand the risks, know your own limitations, and always check trail conditions as they can change quickly.

Content

Welcome

This book is a structured guide that will support you with any planning and preparation tasks needed to successfully complete Sweden's most famous long-distance trail – the 430-kilometre long (267 miles) Kungsleden, or Royal Trail. Often referred to as Europe's last remaining wilderness, this trail will take you on an incredible journey into the heart of Swedish Lapland, where, as far as the eye can see, unfolds an unspoiled land of flower-carpeted birch forest and spectacular glacial valleys. But don't be mistaken in thinking this is a serious Arctic expedition only for hardened trekkers. The relatively low-altitudes, somewhat easy-going terrain, and extensive network of mountain huts and emergency shelters along most of the route make the Kungsleden wholly accessible to a wide range of walkers.

Regardless of whether you plan to tackle the entire route or indeed just a section of the Kungsleden, you still need to plan ahead and go properly equipped and prepared for your hike. Based on our personal experience of hiking the entire route from south to north in just 21 days, this book has been written to give you a better understanding of what to expect. Alongside clear descriptions of the trail, you will find it broken down into manageable stages with suggested itineraries for walkers of all fitness and experience levels. Also included is practical information for all budgets based on wild camping or making use of the Swedish Tourist Association (STF) mountain hut system, or a combination of both.

Traversing some of Sweden's grandest and most dramatic landscapes, where you can simply explore the wilds in undisturbed peace and quiet, you will find that the Kungsleden promises to be a hike very different to any you have experienced before. Its unique elements, such as witnessing daylight at midnight, being woken up to majestic reindeer foraging around your tent, catching a rare glimpse of the Northern Lights dancing up above, and relaxing your muscles at the end of a long day in a wood-fired sauna make this a truly memorable hike. We hope that by reading this book you will feel thoroughly versed in all aspects of this trail and inspired to set off on your own long-distance adventure into the Arctic Circle!

Kungsleden Sign at Lake Riebnes

Introduction

It was as far back as the late nineteenth century that the Swedish Tourist Association conceived the idea of creating a continuous hiking trail in the mountain world of Swedish Lapland. Their vision – that this trail would pass through the most beautiful areas of the Lapone mountains and, thus, become 'the king of trails' or the *Royal Trail*. With limited funds, the first section from Kvikkjokk to Abisko was cleared during the 1920s and, in 1928, without any ceremony or inauguration the name *Kungsleden* appeared for the first time, with the opening of the Kvikkjokk mountain station.

The trail was further extended over several decades and today stretches approximately 430 kilometres (267 miles) from Abisko in the north to Hemavan in the south, where the Vindelfjällen Nature Reserve, one of the largest protected areas in Europe, was created in 1975. Now, not only does the trail cross several lakes of varying size, it also traverses five of Sweden's national parks that comprise a magnificent mosaic of different landscapes, namely Abisko, Pieljekaise, Stora Sjöfallet, Padjelanta, and Sarek. The latter three forming part of the UNESCO World Heritage Site of Laponia.

What also ensued was the development of a well-built system of mountain stations and mountain huts along the majority of the route, thereby making the Kungsleden ever more accessible for the ordinary trail seeker. Completing the full distance can be a demanding undertaking, particularly if you are on a tight itinerary and have to make your miles each day. Yet despite its wild reputation and remote location, this hike is not at all about technical skill. Consider it more a test of your stamina and longevity.

If you are looking for a superb walking holiday that will take you through a changing landscape of forest, valleys, lakes, and mountains with huge, sweeping views of the surrounding wilderness, then the Kungsleden offers just that. But it doesn't have to include a heavy backpack and long legs. Sleeping in the mountain huts, making use of their cooking facilities, and resupplying on the go from boutique shops in the huts, alleviates the need to carry a full backpack of equipment and food rations for the entire trip.

After some initial research into the trail, we knew that the Kungsleden would present us with a beautiful journey through the Scandinavian Mountain Range. Yet for us, choosing this destination for our next long-distance hike was not just about the scenery or the terrain. What really appealed to us was the thought of venturing into the Arctic Circle for the first time, neither of us having ever been so far north in the world. We were also attracted by several unique elements that this trail offers, such as witnessing the midnight sun and indeed the amazing phenomenon of the *aurora borealis* on a clear night.

Figure 1 – Overview Map of the Kungsleden

But by far what firmed up our decision to head east into Scandinavia is Sweden's *Allemansrätten* – the freedom to roam, which is one of our favourite aspects of the Kungsleden. This means that you can legally wild camp anywhere as long as you follow a few simple rules (i.e., leave the surroundings undisturbed and follow the *leave no trace* ethic). Because wild camping is illegal in our home country, England, we were very much looking forward to finding scenic viewpoints where we could set up camp without the worry of being moved on or having to pitch the tent late and leave early the next morning. Our only reservation in terms of camping was the unpredictable mountain weather and real likelihood of rain. But with the option of staying in a comfortable mountain hut at the end of a day's walk if we needed to, we were fully prepared should the weather turn for the worse.

With this book, we provide a clear picture of what you should expect on the Kungsleden, so that you can confidently plan and efficiently prepare for your own wilderness adventure. *Chapter 1* summarises the challenge at hand in terms of physical requirements whilst also providing tools to help you estimate the time and budget needed. *Chapter 2* gives an overview of trail and weather conditions to be expected, points of interest along the route, camping options, water availability, safety notes, as well as animal and plant life. *Chapter 3* discusses trip planning items that generally warrant sufficient lead time, such as travel and transportation links for getting to and from the start and end points. This is not only to potentially save money, but also to ensure that preferred options are available. *Chapter 4* covers specific details on itinerary planning, proper training and nutrition to help you carefully and effectively prepare for your trip. *Chapter 5* provides an overview of essential hiking gear items suitable for the weather and climate of northern Sweden in summer conditions and offers advice on their correct use. Lastly, *Chapter 6* summarises all efforts and considerations that went into our own 21-day journey on the Kungsleden in August/September 2016. These personal accounts are intended to provide inspiration, guidance, and additional reference points.

As well as an immense sense of achievement, on completion of the trail what we came away with were fantastic memories of a place that we had always considered to be both out of our reach and out of our comfort zone. We hope that this book will be a valuable resource for shaping your own wilderness adventure on Sweden's king of trails and that you, too, will have an enjoyable and memorable experience for all the right reasons.

Let the Kungsleden enrich your life. Happy hiking!

Visit *www.PlanAndGoHiking.com* for more information and pictures.

1. Summary of the Challenge

Can you hike the Kungsleden? If you love hiking in pristine wilderness, if you have the stamina for an extensive 430-kilometre (267 miles) multi-day backpacking adventure, and if you have the mental and physical fortitude to endure changeable mountain weather, then the answer is most certainly YES! With the right preparation and attitude, you will find the Kungsleden a satisfying challenge that is more than achievable. All you have to do is plan your adventure carefully and go!

a. Requirements

Venturing north into the Arctic Circle, you would be mistaken if thinking that you must be a serious trekker or hardened wild camper to accomplish this long-distance trail, as there is nothing technically difficult about the route. Even with a full pack and the intention to wild camp, such as ourselves, an average hiker in moderate shape with a taste for adventure and a good set of walking legs can take on the challenge and find they can go the distance.

If you intend on completing the entire 430-kilometre trail, you do need to be reasonably fit and prepared for some long walking days. On a fast paced itinerary, we covered average daily distances of around 25 kilometres (16 miles). The terrain is typically a combination of dense birch or pine forest, opening out into vast, glacial mountain valleys, but the trail is well-defined and easy to follow. With the exception of going over Tjäktja Pass, which is the highest point on the entire Kungsleden at 1,140 metres, you will only be faced with modest height gains and losses from start to finish, so walking is not too rigorous or demanding.

Underfoot, the main hindrances along the way are rocks, roots, and boggy ground, so paying attention to the placement of your feet is a must. Stony sections are long and take some negotiating and can really slow your pace down. However, wooden boardwalks, which are a frequent feature on the Kungsleden, have been put in place in the worst areas to assist you over boggier terrain, also helping to alleviate erosion where hikers go off-trail. There are also bridges across non-fordable streams and, during the summer season, local charter boat services (fee payable) or row-boats (free) are in place, enabling you to get across several large lakes that form part of the trail.

Depending on when you go, the most challenging elements you will encounter will be plagues of mosquitoes and the unpredictable Arctic mountain weather. During the summer season, the tundra is abuzz with large clouds of biting, blood-sucking insects that can bring misery to even the most hardened hiker. Having experienced rain for at least a third of our trip, you should also be prepared for cold, wet weather as the norm.

Water is readily available along the entire trail, so you don't have the additional weight of having to carry several litres along with a full pack of gear. Previously established camp spots with self-made fire rings are also fairly easy to find, usually located near to a water source.

Fully equipped huts and cabins are situated along the route between Hemavan and Ammarnäs and between Kvikkjokk and Abisko. At most huts, you can buy food during the summer season, so if you plan ahead, there is little need to carry more than a day-pack if you intend on overnighting in them. The distance between the huts and cabins does vary, but it is usually between 12 and 15 kilometres (7-9 miles), which is a comfortable day-walk.

There are no STF huts between Ammarnäs and Kvikkjokk, which is a section of the Kungsleden of approximately 130 kilometres (81 miles). If you are intending on completing the entire route, this is where you will need to have your own tent and appropriate sleep gear or, alternatively, make use of private accommodation available in Bäverholmen, Adolfström, Jäkkvik, and Vuonatjviken. Some unmanned emergency shelters can also be found along the route, which are invaluable in extreme weather.

Whilst travelling in Sweden, you will find that the majority of Swedes can converse very well in English. Therefore, learning the Swedish language is not a necessary requirement for your trip. However, knowing a few basic phrases in Swedish is always helpful in daily life situations, such as buying items in grocery stores, ordering food in small restaurants/cafés, and organising transport, such as when phoning ahead to organise the lake crossings that form part of the Kungsleden. Being able to say 'good morning', ask 'how are you', and show courtesy with 'please' and 'thank you' in Swedish will also endear you to the people you meet as you are trying to engage with them in the local language and culture, instead of merely observing it from the edge.

If you intend on staying in Swedish Tourist Association (STF) accommodation along the route, posters, noticeboards, and information booklets that are written in Swedish usually have an English translation alongside them. However, some signs indicating specific facilities such as 'drinking water' or 'toilets' are written in Swedish only, so it may be helpful to recognise these key words. To assist you with this, we have included the most common phrases with their English translations that you will see regularly at mountain huts along the route in Appendix J.

b. Time

Based on our own itinerary of 21 days' hiking, it is possible to complete the Kungsleden in just three weeks, but this is recommended as a fast pace. A more realistic target of completion for an average fit walker is 28 days, as the trail can be conveniently separated into four segments, each representing approximately one week of hiking. You may also want to allow for some spare days to allow for contingencies, should weather conditions, general trail fatigue, or minor injury hamper your progress. Additional days should also be incorporated into your itinerary if you plan on taking side trips or detours off-trail to points of interest, which are discussed later in Chapter 2.

But what time is right for you? The actual time will vary dependent on your age, level of fitness, and overall schedule. Another factor to take into consideration is how much weight you will carry in your backpack as this can affect how far you can walk each day. To have an enjoyable experience with an adequate challenge, start by estimating your days on the trail. Your estimate of trail days (ETD) will help with all your further planning, especially regarding your food and resupply.

The table below is intended to provide guidance for an initial assessment.

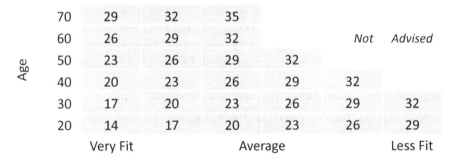

Age	Very Fit		Average			Less Fit
70	29	32	35			
60	26	29	32		Not	Advised
50	23	26	29	32		
40	20	23	26	29	32	
30	17	20	23	26	29	32
20	14	17	20	23	26	29

Level of Fitness

Figure 2 – Estimate of Trail Days

Selecting your age and corresponding fitness level will give you an idea of how long it will approximately take you to complete the trail. For example, a 40-year-old person of average fitness can expect to take roughly 26-29 days to complete the Kungsleden at an enjoyable pace.

Once you have determined your ETD, you can calculate your average daily mileage by dividing the total distance of the Kungsleden by your ETD:

Average kilometres per day = 430 kilometres / ETD

Continuing the above example leads to 430/28 = 15.4 kilometres (9.5 miles) per day on average. This might not sound like much, but keep in mind that unpredictable mountain weather can quickly affect your progress. For example, if severe rain forces you to stop and take shelter in an emergency hut for an afternoon, the next day you may have to double up on sections to maintain your schedule.

There are other trail-specific factors that will affect your timing as well. Where you intend to sleep, whether it be camping in the wilds or at a mountain hut, and whether this coincides with boat schedules for lake crossings (usually twice a day, once in the morning and once early evening) could mean some longer and some shorter days. Furthermore, are you the type of hiker who enjoys:

- Hiking at a relaxed pace?
- Taking frequent or long rest breaks?
- Spending time on photography?
- Taking a cool dip in a mountain lake?
- Having down time in camp to read and journal?
- Taking rest days?
- Having extra time for side trips?

If your answer is yes to any of these questions, you will want to plan a more relaxed itinerary to allow extra time to enjoy these activities. If you cannot answer these questions just yet, don't worry. You may only know whether you would like to spend more time in certain areas after further research. You can always update your estimate later.

We were restricted to a 21-day itinerary due to work commitments. This didn't allow for any zero hiking days, even if we needed them. Most hikers we passed were wowed with our ambition as 28 days is usually considered the minimum number of days for completing the entire Kungsleden. We did, however, pass some fell runners who were managing 30 kilometres (18 miles) a day and aiming to complete the trail in just 14 days!

c. Budget

The Kungsleden is mostly frequented during the summer season, which runs from June to September. Such is the popularity of the trail that prices remain constant throughout this period, so there is no 'off-peak' rate. However, significant discounts with regards to day use of the STF mountain huts, overnight stays, and charter boat services can be obtained on production of an STF or *Hostelling International* card (see Section 3d).

If you are an overseas traveller, your first cost will be getting to and from Sweden. This might not be too expensive if you can fly with a budget airline to Stockholm and make reservations well in advance. Sweden is an affluent country, and we found both the standard of living as well as the price of goods and services to be high compared with what we were used to. So be prepared to pay significantly more for your food and lodging.

Another expense to be considered quite early is the cost of your transport to and from the trail. Buses and trains operate from both Hemavan and Abisko, but if you are time-limited, it may be more convenient to take a domestic flight either to or from Hemavan (or Kiruna), depending on which direction you walk. A money-saving option could be taking an overnight train from Abisko to Stockholm (or vice versa), which will save you the cost of a night's accommodation.

A significant portion of your budget will go on accommodation fees if you are intending on staying in the STF mountain huts and stations along the route. Similarly, if you plan to resupply with food from the shops (*butik*) in the huts, you will be paying up to three times the cost of that purchased from a supermarket. But that's the price of being on a wilderness trail!

The cheapest option is to carry basic food rations after stocking up from a supermarket before you set off on the trail and wild camp as much as possible. You can top up your food supplies from a handful of small supermarkets and shops in the south, but in the northern section you will have no choice but to purchase some food from mountain huts as this is the only option available. (Unless you carry it all from the start, which is a heavy alternative, but we did see several hikers doing this to make the hike more affordable!)

Bear in mind, camping is the most cost-effective choice and lowest budget option, assuming you already own the equipment needed to sleep comfortably in your tent. However, if you have to buy much of the necessary gear, then this will significantly increase your expenses. Even though purchasing brand new gear may put a hefty dent in your budget, investing in thoroughly-researched gear is definitely worth your time and money. Your gear is your life on the trail, but it is also worth remembering that more expensive does not always translate to better!

Boat fees for crossing several of the larger lakes are an additional expense along the trail (see Table 1 below), as is the cost of the bus (77 SEK p/p) that hikers usually take between Kebnats and Vakkotavare, which saves you 30 kilometres (19 miles) of road walking.

Location	Approx. Distance	Boat Type	Operator	Fee
Lake Tjårvekallegiehtje (after Jäkkvik)	0.5km	Row	Norrbotten County Board	Free
Lake Riebnes (to Vuonatjviken)	6km	Motor	Private	300 SEK p/p
Lake Saggat (to Kvikkjokk)	4km	Motor	Private	200 SEK p/p
Lake Laitaure (to Aktse)	3km	Row & motor	STF	200 SEK p/p
Lakes Gåbddåjávrre and Gasskajávrre (Svine to Sitojaure)	4km	Row & motor	Private (Sámi Community)	200 SEK p/p
Saltoluokta to Kebnats	2km	Motor	STF	100 SEK p/p
Lake Teusajaure (to Teusajaure)	1km	Row & motor	STF	100 SEK p/p
Alesjaure Lake (STF Alesjaure to outlet of lake)*	5km	Motor	Private	350 SEK p/p

*Optional boat: The Kungsleden continues up the western side of Lake Teusajaure, but in high summer season, it is possible to take a boat trip across the lake, saving you around 5 kilometres (3 miles) of walking.

Table 1 – Lake Crossings by Boat in South-to-North Direction

You may also find yourself adding on lots of little extras – breakfast buffets when passing mountain stations, an ice-cream or cold drink here and there, souvenirs, laundry. A good idea is to allow yourself a 'slush fund' for any rainy day expenses. This could be opting to stay in a mountain hut because of bad weather or simply allowing yourself a couple of beers at the end of a particularly tough day. It would be a shame not to take advantage of a traditional wood-fired Swedish sauna if you have the option to camp next to one or stay inside a mountain hut in a particularly scenic location.

2. What to Expect

The Kungsleden is a unique hiking trail that has it all: striking scenery, thrilling wildlife encounters, serene campsites, and the joys of solitude. This chapter is intended to give you an impression of the conditions and highlights along the route. You will get a clear picture of what to look forward to and what to look out for when attempting to thru-hike this trail. The information provided will also assist you in choosing appropriate gear and setting realistic goals.

a. Trails & Navigation

Accredited to the Swedish Tourist Association (STF), the official distance of the Kungsleden today is 430 kilometres (267 miles). Yet, depending on where you look, some guides cite the trail as being *'a 500 km-long path taking in Kebnekaise, Sweden's highest mountain, en route'*. To reach Kebnekaise, however, you must take a detour off the Kungsleden, thereby giving rise to the discrepancy. For consistency, all distances used in this book are the official distances given by the STF based on the locations of the mountain huts along the route. Options for including Kebnekaise in your itinerary are discussed later.

Hiking Direction

The preferred direction for hiking the Kungsleden is from north to south, as popular opinion deems that the northernmost section of the trail is the best and most scenic. The 72-kilometre (45 miles) section from Abisko to Singi, therefore, is the most frequented part of the entire route. Not exclusively for thru-hikers on the Kungsleden, this northern section also forms part of a weeklong trip for hikers hoping to summit Kebnekaise (2,099m/6,886 ft.), as Singi is the junction where people divert off the main trail and head to the Kebnekaise mountain station at the foot of Sweden's highest peak. Afterwards, they can terminate their trip at Nikkaluokta, which is served by a main road connecting with Kiruna, instead of rejoining the Kungsleden going south.

[i] The popularity of the northernmost section of the Kungsleden during the height of summer means that overcrowding on the trail can become a real problem. If you're looking for splendid isolation, this may be something to avoid.

Taking such factors into consideration, hiking the Kungsleden in the alternative direction of south to north was much more appealing to us. First and foremost, by starting in the south, we could avoid the caravan of walkers on the Kebnekaise circuit but, more importantly, we would also bypass hordes of hikers taking part in the *Fjällräven Classic* - a huge hiking event that takes place in August ever year, attracting thousands of hikers to the northern part of the Kungsleden.

Hiking south to north was also more favourable as the sun would be on our backs and not in our faces, hence, better for photography and for charging batteries with a solar panel. Furthermore, our bodies would have sufficient time to get accustomed to the rhythms of the trail again, making us fitter and stronger to handle what are considered the tougher sections in the north. As the scenery is also regarded as more spectacular here, by hiking in the alternate direction, it would mean saving the best until last!

Trail Conditions

Considerable stretches of the footpath are well-trodden and virtually flat, making the Kungsleden very accessible and an ideal long-distance walking path for anyone with good general health and a moderate base fitness. In the south, where the Kungsleden is less frequented, you will often find yourself walking on little more than a narrow dirt track that winds its way through the wilderness. Here, there is much less evidence of trail erosion, and you can stride out and set a good pace.

It is the northern section of the trail that has the most arctic and alpine feel of the entire Kungsleden. Here, the majority of your time will be spent above treeline, where you will be surrounded by wild, rocky mountains in every direction. Yet, despite the grand vistas and remote hiking possibilities afforded by the trail, altitude differences are relatively small. Most days on the trail will have moderate height gains and losses of between 200 and 300 metres (660-980 ft.). Except for going over Tjäktja Pass at 1,140m (3,740 ft.), which is the highest point on the entire Kungsleden, walking is not too rigorous or demanding, as much of the trail meanders over open moorland and generally runs along valley floors, following rivers and streams.

Where the trail moves away from the open fells, underfoot is predominantly a combination of forest trails, muddy tracks, stony ground, and some boulder fields, all potentially hazardous when wet, so you do have to pay attention and take care with your footing. Where large areas of rocky or boggy ground make walking difficult, wooden boards/plank walkways tend to be used to make covering the ground more manageable. These boardwalks are a typical feature throughout the trail, particularly in the north, where the Kungsleden receives more foot traffic.

Figure 3 – Typical Wooden Boardwalks over Bog | Trail Erosion & Multitude of Pathways

[!•] As excellent as the boardwalks can be at preventing you from getting wet feet, many are in need of maintenance up and down the trail. Broken, dislodged, or slippery boards should be avoided, as they are the main cause of minor injury for hikers on the Kungsleden.

Local counties have the responsibility of maintaining the trail. The County Board of Norrbotten (Länsstyrelsen Norrbotten) covers the largest area of the Kungsleden and is therefore responsible for the upkeep of the majority of it. Several sections in the north have undergone repair, evident with the installation of new boardwalks between Alesjaure and Abisko and the provision of new bridges to support with crossing fast-flowing waterways. However, restoration work is a costly ongoing process. The impacts associated with large numbers of hikers on the trail, coupled with a lack of maintenance, means that some sections farther from the popular trailheads are now suffering with severe erosion, which has increased the difficulty of hiking in some of these parts.

One such example is the section beyond Riebnes Lake, heading north towards Kvikkjokk, where there are large open areas of boggy ground. Unlike other sections of the trail, at the time of our thru-hike, there was a distinct lack of wooden boards to help us across this area. We had no alternative but to wade straight through the bog, resulting in wet boots and soggy feet, which until they had dried out somewhat, made walking very uncomfortable. As much of the length of the trail meanders through broad valley bottoms, you should be prepared for traversing wet, boggy ground for a good portion of your trip.

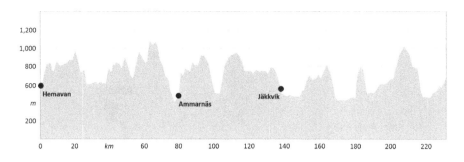

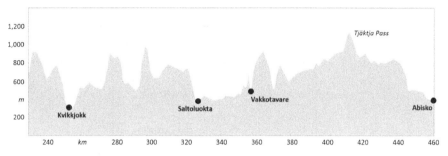

Figure 4 – Elevation Profile of the Kungsleden (South to North)

- *Highest Point:* Tjäktja Pass at 1,140 metres (3,740 feet)
- *Lowest Point:* Kvikkjokk at 305 metres (1,000 feet)

In terms of overall trail difficulty, the Kungsleden is graded as *moderate* largely due to the modest height gains and losses over the course of the trail. However, whilst the walking is not too tough, completing 430 kilometres is a very big undertaking, so you should have previous experience of long-distance walking and be in relatively good physical shape to get the most from this hike. Even if you intend on using STF accommodation for the majority of your overnight stays, remember you will still need to carry food, a sleeping bag, and other essentials, which can affect your walking capabilities in terms of speed, daily mileage, and overall progress along the trail.

Trail Access

The official start and end points of the Kungsleden are *Abisko* in the north and *Hemavan* in the south, but it is possible to join or exit the trail from other settlements along the route that are serviced by road. From north to south these are: Abisko, Nikkaluokta (if you detour to Kebnekaise), Vakkotavare, Saltoluokta, Kvikkjokk, Jäkkvik, Ammarnäs, and Hemavan. All of these locations offer accommodation, resupply, parking, and restrooms.

The convenience of multiple entry and exit points along the trail allows for the choice of spending just a few days, for example between Jäkkvik and Ammarnäs, or an entire month hiking from Hemavan to Abisko.

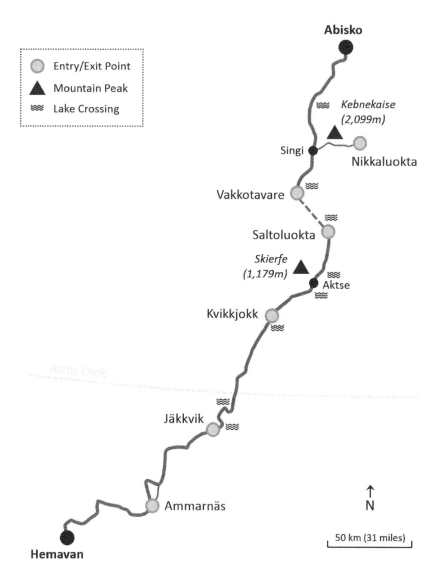

Figure 5 – Kungsleden Entry & Exit Points

Starting in the North

The favoured start point for most hikers is Abisko in the north, which is divided into two areas. The main Abisko village is located around the train station Abisko Östra. However, the Kungsleden starts two kilometres further west opposite the large hotel/hostel Abisko Turiststation, which is next to the train station of the same name. The trailhead is denoted with a large wooden overhead sign, situated at the entrance point to Abisko National Park.

Many hikers arrive by train and stay at the Turiststation the night prior to starting their thru-hike, so they can make final preparations. Alternatively, if you have your food provisions ready, it is possible to take the night train from Stockholm, get off in Abisko, and begin hiking the Kungsleden directly from the train.

Starting in the South

If starting from Hemavan in the south, the Kungsleden is signposted from the centre of town, but the actual trailhead is not so easy to find. It is located above the town in the direction of the ski lifts, next to the Naturum Visitor Centre. Depending on when you arrive, as with Abisko, you may need to spend a night in Hemavan prior to starting your hike to allow time for any final preparations, e.g., visiting the supermarket for food and gas.

Trail Sections

The Kungsleden is traditionally split into *four stages*. (There is an additional stage if you wish to include the detour to Kebnekaise). Travelling in the direction of south to north, as this is how we completed the thru-hike, the route is described below:

Stage 1: Hemavan to Ammarnäs (5-6 days; 78km/48.5 miles)

This is considered the easiest part of the trail and is well facilitated with STF huts and emergency shelters at regular intervals, generally within one-day walking distances of each other. Here, you will pass over low fells and heather-covered moors, through birch forests and wetlands, the horizon lined with impressive fell peaks. The Kungsleden officially begins (or ends) in the ski-resort town of Hemavan, which is situated along the valley of the Ume river. Sprawling between Hemavan and Ammarnäs is the largest natural reserve in Sweden – the Vindel Mountain Nature Reserve (*Vindelfjällen*), also one of the largest protected areas in Europe.

To reach the 'official' Kungsleden trailhead, follow signs from the main street in Hemavan that direct you uphill towards the ski lifts and the Naturum Visitor Centre, which overlooks the town. The start of the trail is located to the right of the building, denoted with a large wooden archway that says *Kungsleden* overhead. From here, the trail weaves its way through silver birch forest, then heads straight up into the mountains, following alongside the trickling Syterbäcken river. Here, you will be walking along a verdant valley floor with extremely steep mountain sides, as you are surrounded with peaks of more than 1,700 metres (5,580 feet). One of them, Norra Sytertoppen (1,768m/5,800 ft.), is an easy traverse, so hikers often take this path as an alternate route between the mountain huts of Viter and Syter to summit a peak along the way.

Figure 6 – Boggy Section of Trail | Lake Tärnasjö

On the Kungsleden, after 11 kilometres (6.8 miles), the first STF hut that you will reach is Viterskalsstugan, situated at the west end of the U-shaped Syterskalet valley. This makes a good lunch stop if you intend on continuing 12 or so kilometres (7 miles) further along the trail to the Syter hut, which lies next to the Svärfar river in northern Storfjället. If you need to seek refuge indoors because of bad weather, partway between the STF huts is the Syterskalet emergency shelter. Continuing beyond the STF Syter hut, you will use a network of bridges to cross various lakes in what is called the Tärnasjö archipelago. From the southern end of Lake Tärnasjö, the trail winds east along the lake for several kilometres before reaching the Tärnasjö STF hut. With beautiful views across the lake, this a perfect place to relax and experience your first Swedish sauna and to make an overnight stop either camping or staying inside the hut.

The next 14 kilometres (9 miles) of trail leading to the Serve STF mountain hut is over heather-covered moors on good track, allowing you to pick up the pace and make good time. There is an impressive view straight down the valley where distant snow-capped peaks whet the appetite for what is to come. Beyond Serve, the remaining 25 kilometres (15.5 miles) to Ammarnäs is mostly above the treeline. While the ascent is gradual and not too demanding, there is some rough walking over large stone boulders at times. As this section of the trail is very exposed, you may also face high winds and a drop in temperature. If caught out in bad weather, you could seek refuge in the Vuomatjåhkka or Juovvatjåhkka (also known as Aigert) huts along this section. With an A-frame structure, they are very simple, emergency shelters, furnished with a cast iron stove and a couple of wooden benches to sit/sleep on.

The Kungsleden then skirts the peaks of Juovvatjåhkka (1,112m/3,648 ft.) and Uhtsa-Ájgart (1,076m/3,530 ft.), before descending over 200 metres to a grassy plateau where the Aigert STF hut is located. Take a rest break here and enjoy 360- degree panoramic views of the surrounding lakes and forested peaks, after which you will be faced with a steep descent when tackling the final 8 kilometres (5 miles) of trail leading to Ammarnäs. If it has been raining, the ground will be wet and slippery, making for a particularly tough downhill walk, so pay careful attention to your footing. With a population of less than 300, the tiny mountain village of Ammarnäs is the first settlement you will reach after leaving Hemavan. It is located beside the Gautsträsk lake in a wide river valley at the foot of the Ammarfjället mountains. This is a good place to resupply, as there is a well-provisioned supermarket in the centre of town.

Stage 2: Ammarnäs to Kvikkjokk (8-10 days; 165km/102.5 miles)

Note: Hike can be split off or out of Jäkkvik or Adolfström.

This section of the Kungsleden is characterised by long swathes of forest and numerous mountain crossings, as the trail travels from valley to valley. Not recommended for novices, it is considered one of the most difficult stretches of the Kungsleden, as distances between mountain huts can be long and there are three lakes to cross. Its redeeming feature is that it is one of the quietest sections of trail. Several smaller communities, cabins, and cottages give the area a character of its own, unlike other parts of Kungsleden. From Ammarnäs, there's a choice of two routes: 55 kilometres (34 miles) direct to Adolfström or 23 kilometres (14 miles) to the Rävfallsstugan cabin, which is situated close to a three-metre waterfall on the Rävfallet river, continuing a further 49 kilometres (30 miles) to Adolfström.

Whichever route you take, part of your time will be spent walking along the Vindelälven river valley, one of Sweden's richest fishing grounds for grayling and sea trout. A short hike uphill through birch forest is followed by vast sections of open moorland. Here, you can stride out and make good time as the trail is flat and well-trodden. Walk along an elongated ridge and enjoy extensive lakeland views as you continue north on the trail to the Sjnulttjie shelter. You can break up the day by camping here for free or take refuge in the shelter in bad weather. Soon, you will leave the bare mountain region behind and descend into forest. With an abundance of wild flowers and a woodland floor rich in mushrooms, this is a good section to see undisturbed flora and fauna typical of northern Sweden.

Figure 7 – Route Options from Ammarnäs | Crossing Vindel River

If you are already in need of some home comforts before reaching Adolfström, take advantage of Bäverholmen, a lesser-known settlement that can only be reached on foot or by boat, which offers private accommodation, camping, and a restaurant/café. From Bäverholmen, walk around the shores of Iraft lake or, alternatively, pay to take a private motor boat across the lake to save yourself 5 kilometres (3 miles) and a couple of hours walking on rocky trail that can be hard-going on your feet. Stay overnight in Adolfström at a private cabin or campsite before continuing to Jäkkvik.

This section of the Kungsleden crosses the Pieljekaise National Park, where you will be walking through herb-rich mountain birch forest. Although there are no STF huts along this section of the trail, there is a shelter and a cabin provided by the County Administrative Board of Norrbotten. As Jäkkvik can be reached by car, it makes a good exit/entry point if you intend on hiking just a section of the Kungsleden. It is also a good place to resupply, as there is a garage and small supermarket. Additionally, if you want a break from camping, there is an excellent church hostel with dorm beds priced less than at the STF huts.

A few kilometres after leaving Jäkkvik, you will encounter your first boat crossing over the Tjårvekallegiehtje lake. (At the very north-western end of the large Lake Hornavan.) It is a short distance of 500 metres (1,640 ft.), with rowing boats provided free of charge. After rowing across the lake, you will be walking on a forest trail for several kilometres, part of which goes through dense vegetation, where some burdensome rocks and roots may slow down your pace.

The trail then gently heads uphill and moves out of the treeline, skirting around the Tjidtjakválle peak, a modest mountain at 793 metres (2,600 feet). Descending around 200 metres to the edge of Lake Riebnes, you must take private transport across the vast lake to the holiday village of Vuonatjviken, where the Kungsleden then continues. Coming from the south, it is recommended that you phone ahead from Jäkkvik to pre-arrange transport and agree departure times with the skipper residing in Vuonatjviken. Otherwise, it is possible you may lose a hiking day waiting for the boat as there isn't a set schedule.

Figure 8 – Private Motor Boat across Riebnes Lake | Suspension Bridge over Bartek River

Once on the other side of Lake Riebnes, you can stay in a private cabin at Vuonatjviken or continue along the Kungsleden, following a birch forest track for around 5 kilometres (3 miles), after which you should find some good camping spots along tributaries of the Bartek river. From Vuonatjviken, it is around 30 kilometres (19 miles) before you will reach any further lodging. If you enjoy lakeside walking, the next 10 kilometres (6 miles) or so is a particularly beautiful section of the Kungsleden. You will cross several outlets, where the lakes and rivers diverge and your attention is drawn to endless sections of still, calm waters with stunning lake reflections, providing some excellent photographic opportunities.

The walk gets a little more demanding from here, because the trail meanders up and down between river valleys and plateaus, which have a few hundred metres height difference. Climb out of the forest and over the Barturtte plateau, which, at just over 1000 metres (3,280 feet), offers a splendid view over the surrounding moorlands. Blending in with the Arctic tundra, you will pass a traditional grass-covered Lappish hut that can provide respite in the event of severe wind and rain.

Descending towards Tjieggelvas lake, the vegetation gets thicker and the trail gets boggier. There are several sections that need replacement boardwalks, so be prepared for wet feet! The Kungsleden then veers around the north-western end of the lake where there is a large suspension bridge across the outlet flowing into Lake Fálesjávrre. We found this to be the worst section of the entire Kungsleden for mosquitoes and biting insects, so promptly put on our head nets and covered up every inch of bare skin.

Leaving the extensive waterways and blood-sucking pests behind, the trail winds upwards through birch woodland, opening out onto a vast plateau covered in wild blueberries. Huge, craggy peaks dominate the skyline up ahead, as the trail rises sharply, then descends over a boulder field and through a narrow valley between the Sjpietjam mountains. Covering 55 kilometres (34 miles) since setting off from Vuonatjviken, you will be grateful of a rest break in the Tsielekjåkk hut. This is an unstaffed hut with two beds that can be used in the event of emergency and/or as a shelter in severe weather. There is also a telephone should you need to make an emergency call.

Leave the hut and rejoin the Kungsleden on a clear forest track. After several kilometres of woodland walking, the trail winds its way sharply downhill to Lake Saggat. Here, you will need to take a private motor boat across the lake to reach the modest village of Kvikkjokk. Boats generally run twice a day, but when hiking northbound, you are advised to phone ahead to pre-arrange transportation. If you can't get a cell phone signal, there is access to a phone from the boatman's cabin on the lakeshore.

Kvikkjokk is a main entry/exit point of the Kungsleden as there are daily buses to and from Jokkmokk, a small town in the east, situated on the main E45 road, with onward connections to Sweden's main cities. STF accommodation in Kvikkjokk is a fully-equipped Fjällstation, meaning you can have a hot shower, get laundry done, and take advantage of the restaurant by having an evening meal and all-you-can-eat buffet breakfast. The hostel also provides free Wi-Fi for guests.

Stage 3: Kvikkjokk to Saltoluokta (4-6 days; 73km/45 miles)

Note: A detour can be taken to Skierfe and into Sarek National Park.

This segment of the Kungsleden passes through a bare landscape edged by pine and birch forests and involves crossing two lakes. Leave Kvikkjokk on a steady uphill climb through old, coniferous forests consisting of spruce and pine. The track is well-trodden and easy-going, except for the slopes surrounding the ancient gathering place Tingstallstenen, as the path may turn into a creek with persistent rain. After 16 kilometres (10 miles), you will reach the STF Pårte hut, which makes a good lunch stop. There are several scenic camp spots around the Sjabttjakjávrre lake next to the hut, but you are required to pay a fee to the STF if you camp anywhere on the shoreline.

After leaving the hut, you will pass through beautiful pine forest, reputedly one of the few untouched pine primeval forests in Lapland. Navigating can be a little tricky in the rain, but you will soon be above the treeline skirting the Bårddegiehtje mountains. You can use the rowing boats provided to row across Lake Laitaure or take a motor boat operated by the STF. The STF Aktse hut is located on the northern side of the lake, 24 kilometres (15 miles) from Pårte. If approaching from the south, you need to hang the white flag located on the jetty to signal that you would like transportation across the lake, as there are not always hikers travelling southbound late in the day for you to take a return boat.

Leave the jetty on the northern shore of Lake Laitaure and walk a couple of kilometres across the wetlands, making use of the wooden planks laid down here, leading to the Aktse mountain farm area, where the STF has two cabins. Located along the Rapa valley, the STF Aktse facilities are approximately halfway between Kvikkjokk and Saltoluokta, making this an excellent place for taking some side trips off the Kungsleden. From here, you can make day trips into Sarek National Park, learn of the Sámi and mountain farmers' cultural history, or just enjoy the tranquillity and beautiful surroundings, particularly in summer, when the vast meadows become carpeted in bright yellow buttercups.

Beyond here, this segment of the Kungsleden sees you moving in an exciting borderland between Sarek's sharp ridges and towering peaks of granite, contrasted with lush, dark green forest scenery to the east. With limited mapped trails, Sarek National Park is the largest high mountain area in the country and remains a piece of true wilderness. The Kungsleden runs through the southern part of the park for a stretch of 16 kilometres (10 miles), with the closest STF huts being Pårte and Aktse. From Aktse, taking a detour to the summit of Skierfe right on the edge of the park will provide you with perhaps the best view in Sweden, as you look across the meandering milky rivers of the Rapadalen (Rapa valley) 600 metres below. It is a hefty climb to get above treeline but well worth earmarking a day in your itinerary to do this in good weather just for the magnificent vista you will experience!

Figure 9 – Row Boats to Cross Lake Laiture | Sarek National Park

If you do not make the detour, it is 13 kilometres (8 miles) from Aktse to the next STF hut, Sitojaure, starting with a steep, uphill climb from the valley floor of around 300 metres. Once you gain height, the trail then seems to flatten out for a while as you cross the extensive Njunjes plateau covered in stunted Arctic scrub. Although the ground can be rocky in places, much of the trail underfoot is compacted soil and relatively easy-going. Before you begin descending, you will pass a sign telling you to phone ahead to arrange boat transport across the mountain lakes Gåbddåjávrre and Gasskajávrre, (known generally as Lake Sitojaure), as there is limited cell phone coverage beyond this point.

Pass through scattered birch forest as you head down to the lakeside on an easy walking trail. There is a shelter by the pier, Svijnne, where you can rest and wait for the boat. The lakes are shallow, making it possible to row across. However, it is recommended that you take the motor boat operated by local Sámi people, as the lakes can be very choppy in strong wind. On the northern side of the lakes, you will find the STF hut Sitojaure. This hut has limited facilities, i.e., there is no shop. However, it is sometimes possible to buy basic supplies, such as bread and fish, from the nearby Sámi community at Tjåhke (1.6-km/1-mile detour). From Tjåhke, it is also possible to take a boat tour west along Lake Sitojaure to Rinim and enter Sarek National Park from here.

After leaving Sitojaure, you will cross bare fells covered in ripris, a low growing Arctic shrub that, as autumn takes hold, changes to a deep, striking red. Now looking to the west, you will be met with a grand mountain view. Here, the Kungsleden runs through the Áutsutjvágge valley, below the imposing peaks of Sjäksjos (1,250m) and the steep-sided Njalásjbákte (1,091m). As there is little variation in height, this section of the trail presents an opportunity for striding out and covering good ground in a relatively short time. About halfway, take a break at Áutsutjvágge shelter before the long descent to the STF Saltoluokta mountain station, situated a few hundred metres from the lake with the same name. After what seems like a never-ending section of trail, it finally winds downhill through pine forest for around 3 kilometres (2 miles), before changing into a woodland of willow and birch, where the cabins of the Saltoluokta Fjällstation come into view.

Figure 10 – Njunjes Plateau towards Lake Sitojaure | Saltoluokta Fjällstation

The original STF accommodation was built here in 1912, with further cabins added to provide for increased visitor numbers. The current Fjällstation resembles an up-market mountain lodge, catering to weekend visitors and tour groups, not just hikers on the Kungsleden. It is renowned on the trail for serving the best 3-course evening meal, so most hikers include it in their itinerary as an overnight stop. The main building houses a restaurant, shop, and reception, with some bedrooms on the first floor. Hikers tend to camp or stay in cabins across from the main building. Saltoluokta makes a good entry/exit point if you are considering tackling only a section of the Kungsleden, as there are public transport connections to Gällivare and Kiruna.

Stage 4: Saltoluokta to Abisko (4-7 days; 111km/70 miles)

Note: + 30km (19 miles) bus journey from Kebnats to Vakkotavare.

From Saltoluokta heading north, you can take off your walking boots and relax a while, as continuing on the Kungsleden requires a boat ride and bus journey before you hit the trail again. Take the early morning boat across Saltoluokta lake to Kebnats, where a connecting bus will be waiting to transport you 30 or so kilometres (19 miles) to Vakkotavare (fee payable). Between Kebnats and Vakkotavare, the Kungsleden is missing a long section of trail, so most hikers pay and take the bus rather than walking the distance on asphalt.

The next STF hut is Vakkotavare, located opposite Suorvajaure Lake, right next to the highway, opposite the parking area where the bus drops you off. This main road leads to Ritsem, where there is another STF hut and Sámi camp. If you want a break from the Kungsleden, or to terminate your trip here, Ritsem is an excellent starting point for hiking and skiing in the Áhkká massif and for exploring the Sarek and Padjelanta National Parks.

After a brief encounter with civilisation, rejoin the Kungsleden and head back into the wilderness. The trail starts with quite a gruelling 2-kilometre (1.2 miles) steep uphill climb past the Vakkotavare hut, crossing a bridge over a cascading waterfall. Don't forget to turn around and enjoy the view of Lake Suorvajaure from up high. With a bit of effort, it is not long before you are above the treeline and standing on a highland plateau, looking upon several towering snow-capped peaks within the Stora Sjöfallet National Park. Rich in nutrients, vitamins, and antioxidants, this is a good place to take a rest and sample some wild blueberries picked fresh from the brushwood to give you a burst of energy before continuing on the trail.

From Vakkotavare it is 16 kilometres (10 miles) to the next STF hut, Teusajaure. After reaching the plateau, you will be walking on a well-trodden track that weaves its way through the Arctic scrub. The route is very clear, even if visibility is low, as large cairns are positioned at either side of the track at regular intervals. Along this section, there are several streams that bisect the trail, which do not have wooden planks or bridges to support you with crossing. However, the water channels are littered with stones and boulders, so you can negotiate each crossing with a careful rock hop. As you continue north, look out for reindeer foraging along the grassy slopes before heading downhill towards the lake.

Before reaching the STF hut, Lake Teusajaure must be crossed. Rowing boats are available, but, as an alternative, the host at the STF hut provides transportation for a fee. As it is only a short distance of around a kilometre, crossing Lake Teusajaure is a relatively easy row if you want to save money.

[!] If you use the rowing boats provided at any lake crossing along the Kungsleden, be aware that you must leave at least one boat on each side of the lake. This means that if there is only one boat on your side, then you must row across the lake, then back again with two boats, leave one, and return, in effect, crossing the lake three times!

Figure 11 – Bus Transport from Kebnats to Vakkotavare | Waterfall past Lake Teusajaure

The STF hut Teusajaure is beautifully located right on the edge of the lake at the foot of the Slieknjamačohkka mountainside (1,730m/5,676 ft.). Camp overnight by the lake and enjoy morning reflections of the bulbous Gáppetjåhkkå peak (1,457m/4,780 ft.), looking across Lake Teusajaure to the west. Rejoin the Kungsleden heading straight uphill through green slopes of mountain birch and ancient pine forest, passing beside a large waterfall that you will see crashing down the steep hillside. This is the big climb of the day, after which you will reach a highland plateau. Take a breather and enjoy the tremendous view, looking back across the lake to the high peaks in the Stora Sjöfallet National Park.

The plateau can be very wet with large parts of the path flooded. From here on, the trail is also very rocky and churned up in places, needing you to watch every step and take care with your footing. After about a kilometre, you will pass a small wooden sign saying "BRO", which means *bridge*. To reach the bridge, it will mean taking a short detour off the Kungsleden that will add an extra kilometre or so to your day. If you are short on time or reluctant to walk the additional distance, assess the water level at the time of your crossing and use the large boulders as stepping stones if safe to do so. The largest river on this section, Kaitumjåkka, has a large suspension bridge in place to see you safely across. From Teusajaure, it is just 9 kilometres (5.5 miles) until you will reach Kaitumjaure, the next STF hut. This hut is a great place to stock up with food for the rest of your journey north, as it has the largest boutique shop so far on the trail (not including the Fjällstations). Kaitumjaure is also one of the best places to see more elusive wildlife on your hike, as there is a resident moose that can often be spotted wandering in the lakeside marches below the hut.

This next segment of the Kungsleden takes you through birch forest, open fells, and deep valleys, all with impressive views of the surrounding peaks. From Kaitumjaure, it is a long valley walk due north on a stony but flat trail that runs alongside the fast-flowing Tjäktjajåkka river. A large suspension bridge takes you across the river where the Kungsleden continues on the eastern side. Make the most of this section, being one of the quieter places, as beyond Singi, the trail becomes much busier, especially during the height of summer. Up until now, for the most part, you will have probably only passed a handful of people on the trail each day, with the huts being slightly busier at night. From here on in, you will see a huge difference in the amount of foot traffic. As the STF hut at Singi is part of the Kebnekaise loop, you may also find that overcrowding is an issue. To avoid this and maintain your wilderness experience, make camp either a little way before or after the hut, where it will be much quieter in the valley.

[i] If you choose to include the Kebnekaise loop in your itinerary, this would be considered an additional stage, whereby you need to allow at least an extra couple of days. Generally, hikers complete the 52 kilometres (32 miles) from Saltoluokta to Kebnekaise in 3 days. Allow an extra day if you intend on making a trip to the summit. Even then, as the weather conditions are so unpredictable, you may find it is not possible to make the ascent, despite careful planning and preparation. To complete the northern section of the Kungsleden, the final 87 kilometres (54 miles) from Kebnekaise to Abisko can then be undertaken in 5 to 6 days.

If you want to attempt an ascent of Kebnekaise, on reaching the Singi STF hut, you can choose to take a side trail to the east, following the Lássajávri river along the Láddjuvággi valley for 14 kilometres (8.5 miles), where the Kebnekaise Fjällstation is located below the peak of Sweden's highest mountain. From the mountain station, you can book a guided tour taking you to the summit. A guided walk in the Tarfala valley is another popular excursion if you have a few spare days. The side track doesn't terminate at the Fjällstation. Rather, it continues through the forest to the village Nikkaluokta, which has connecting transport with Kiruna, making it possible to end your thru-hike here. If you do not want to hike all the way to Nikkaluokta, you can shorten the walking distance by taking a boat across the mountain lake Láddjujávri (also known as Ladtjojaure). Similarly, there is the option of taking a helicopter between Kebnekaise and Nikkaluokta, which is why the mountain station also receives a lot of weekend visitors.

If you wish to rejoin the Kungsleden and continue north, you can circle Kebnekaise in a counter-clockwise direction by taking a backcountry trail through the Darfálvággi valley 8 kilometres (5 miles) to the STF Tarfala hut. The Tarfala Research Station is located about one kilometre from here, which studies the glaciers and climate change in the area. Note, that the trail gets steeper and more strenuous as the hut is located 1,100 metres above sea level at the foot of the Darfáljávri glacial lake. Beyond the hut, the trail skirts around the lake on the eastern side and continues up a narrow rocky ridge to the right side of the glacier. It then passes the smaller Gaskkasjávri tarn, where you can either head southwest alongside Lake Guobirjávrrit, and along the Guobirjohka river, rejoining the Kungsleden just past the bridge north of the Kuoperjåkka shelter. Or, alternatively, there is a trail that continues north of the Gaskkasjávri tarn to the Gaskkasvággi range, where the trail then makes a southwest turn, following the Gaskkasjohka river. Taking this alternative route, you will rejoin the Kungsleden around halfway along the Tjäktjavagge valley, a few kilometres south of the Sälka STF hut.

[!] Hiking around the Kebnekaise massif will effectively save you a day of time, as the distance is approximately 18 kilometres (11 miles), compared with 34 kilometres (21 miles) if you return to Singi via Kebnekaise, taking your original path. However, these options are both high mountain routes and are only recommended for very experienced hikers, as the trails are unmarked, requiring good navigational skills.

The Kebnekaise massif is Sweden's highest alpine area. Therefore, Tarfala is the STF's highest mountain hut. Here, you will be surrounded by glaciers, towering peaks, and beautiful mountain lakes. The area is particularly exposed, so carefully consider weather and glacier conditions. You will be walking along narrow rocky ridges and may have to cross several ice sheets. Speak to a guide at the Kebnekaise Fjällstation about current conditions before deciding on this option to rejoin the Kungsleden. If in doubt, follow the trail back to Singi along the Láddjuvággi valley on which you came. Alternatively, from Nikkaluokta you could hike 34 kilometres (21 miles) to the Vistas STF hut, then a further 18 kilometres (11 miles) to Alesjaure to get you back on the Kungsleden.

Staying on the Kungsleden: From Singi it is a beautiful 12-kilometre (7.5 miles) walk to Sälka through the long and scenic Tjäktjavagge valley. Here, there are plenty of streams to drink from and wonderful spots to take a rest. The path crawls forward in zigzags but is heavily worn and muddy in places, as it receives much more foot traffic than in the south. Partway take a rest break at the Kuoperjåkka emergency shelter, which offers a short period of relief from heavy wind and rain. In good weather, sit outside the shelter and enjoy the tremendous view down the valley before looking upon the snow-clad northern peak of Kebnekaise to the east.

Figure 12 – Detour off Kungsleden to Kebnekaise | View from Tjaktja Pass

From the STF Sälka hut, it is a further 12 kilometres (7.5 miles) to the Tjäktja STF hut, which lies on a barren slope just off the Kungsleden to the left side of the creek. Now heading through the long and lush Tjäktjajåkka valley, the trail gets rockier, requiring you to watch your footing. You will find there are some boardwalks to assist you across the worst sections, but take care as some are broken in places. From striding out along the valley floor, you will now head uphill to the top of the Tjäktja Pass. At 1,140m metres (3,740 feet), it is the highest point on the Kungsleden and possibly the most strenuous section of trail. As the wind funnels through the pass, expect it to feel much colder. Take respite in the emergency shelter located at the top before continuing north.

On the other side of the Tjäktja Pass stretches a fascinating and unique moonscape. The trail now meanders through the Alisvággi for 13 kilometres (8 miles) with rolling mountains to the west and the alpine landscape towards the Kebnekaise range to the south and east. It can be tiresome and slow-going at first navigating your way across the sprawling jagged boulder field. Several kilometres crossing this terrain can be very wearing on your feet, so make the most of where boardwalks have been placed over the rocks by striding out for a short while. Having gradually descended around

300 metres, the final stretch to the next STF mountain hut, Alesjaure, is easy walking through grassy moors where there are many streams to drink from. You will soon be able to see the cabins in the distance perched high on a mountain ridge overlooking Lake Alesjaure. You will not have to pay a fee if you decide to camp before crossing the swing bridge over the river. However, as Alesjaure is the largest of the STF mountain huts complete with sauna, café, and shop, you may wish to pay for camping close to the hut to make use of these extra facilities.

From Alesjaure, the Kungsleden heads north along the western side of the lake 20 kilometres (12.5 miles) to Abiskojaure. Here, the terrain is flatter than before and the interlocking lakes on the right-hand side dominate the landscape. During the peak season, it is possible to take a boat ride 5 kilometres or so (3 miles) across the lake to save you some walking time, although the trail conditions along the shores side are fairly good. Partway along the lake, there is a side trail leading across the marshy scrub to the Rádunjárga emergency shelter. As the ground is very boggy and the side trail not very well trodden here, it is only worth diverting off the Kungsleden to the shelter in the event of heavy rain or an emergency. Willow shrubs and mountain moors now edge the trail.

This final section of the Kungsleden is characterised by high altitude meadows, grassy fells, jagged rocks, and craggy peaks in every direction. This is mountain walking at its best! Low-growing, bushy willow and dwarf-birch carpet the mountainsides, as you make your way through the verdant Gárdden valley. The towering peak of Gárddenvárri (1,154m/3,786 ft.) will come into view before you begin a gradual descent of around 300 metres, where the trail then winds downhill through woodland, across a suspension bridge over the Ŝiellajohka river and past a designated camping area before entering Abisko National Park. A little further along the trail, the STF Abiskojaure hut is located on the other side of a suspension bridge at the southwestern end of Lake Abiskojaure.

[i] Abisko National Park is the only area of the Kungsleden where wild camping is prohibited. You must either camp before entering the park, camp or stay at the STF hut, or continue further along the trail to another designated camping area, Nissonjokk, located just a few kilometres before Abisko.

Leaving the bare mountain region behind, the final 15 kilometres (9 miles) from Abiskojaure to Abisko can be covered quickly as the Kungsleden follows the Abiskojåkka river. Here, the ground is well-trodden and flat, the trail winding its way through the elongated Abisko National Park. This section contains some of the lushest and most dense vegetation of the trail, the shady birch forest offering a wonderful break from the open, windy mountain moors. Extra-wide boardwalks take you over boggier ground, also making it easier for hikers wanting to pass from alternate directions.

Figure 13 – Blue Skies over Gárdden Valley | Lush Vegetation along Abiskojåkka River

The final 3.5 kilometres (2 miles) become quite a muddy trudge due to the impact of large numbers of visitors using the trail in their exploration of Abisko National Park. After heavy rain, flooding worsens the conditions of this section, so take care as the ground can be very slippery. You will now pass through a limestone canyon with a series of gushing waterfalls presenting a good photographic opportunity along the Abiskojåkka river, which eventually flows into Lake Torneträsk in Abisko.

The finish line is the wooden arch marking the end (or beginning if starting in the other direction) of the Kungsleden. It is located next to the train station Abisko Turiststation and just 300 metres from the STF Abisko mountain station, where, if you have completed the full 430 kilometres, you will want to toast your success with a drink from the bar!

While the Kungsleden in its entirety remains an epic journey and an incredible experience for the long-distance walker, some people may prefer to walk sections of the trail at a time. With several entry/exit points along the route, it is possible to choose any of the stages described above and make them into a one- or two-week walking holiday.

If solitude is what you're looking for, walking the southern section between Hemavan and Ammarnäs may suit your preferences better than the busier northern section. However, if you want grand mountain views and beautiful valley walks, plus the opportunity to summit Sweden's highest peak, then the northernmost section between Abisko and Singi, taking in Kebnekaise and terminating at Nikkaluokta, may offer you a better flavour of Arctic Sweden. More details and further options to help you decide on what itinerary is right for you are included in Appendix C.

Navigation & Maps

The Kungsleden is a clearly defined trail throughout, with good signage at trail junctions and clear waymarks to support you with navigation. Typically, at regular intervals along the trail, rocks and trees are marked with orange/red paint flashes, and signage indicates how many kilometres to the next mountain hut in both directions.

As the Kungsleden is a ski trail in winter, at times, you may find there are two choices of path to follow, as the ski trail takes a slightly different route. Signposts will indicate which is the walking trail and which is the ski trail with a picture symbol of two hikers or a person on skis. So it remains visible in heavy snow, the ski route is easily identifiable by large wooden poles with red crosses running at intervals alongside the track. On the Calazo maps we used, the ski route is shown as long dashed lines, indicating a well-defined trail for winter use only. The hiking trail in comparison is shown as a continuous line of small dots that are close together. This signals a well-defined trail for summer use only.

Figure 14 – Trail Sign & Red Paint on Tree | Hiking Route vs. Ski Route

[!] Whilst it is tempting to follow the ski route in places where the walking route crosses a lot of boggy ground, it is not recommended as the ski route generally takes you over lakes and streams that would be frozen in winter, so you may find yourself well off route and having to backtrack to cross watercourses that are flowing in summer.

As the Kungsleden is so well signposted and the trail well-trodden, even in the south, navigation is almost never an issue unless the weather is extreme. However, it is essential that a map and compass form part of your kit when walking any long-distance trail for safety reasons. Not only is a map vital to support you on your journey, it can also be a useful tool during the planning process. The wealth of information that a map provides can ultimately help you to decide on your own itinerary, as you can see exactly what options are available.

One place on the trail where having a map proved particularly useful for us was the section between Ammarnäs and Adolfström, as there are two route options. The shorter of the two is more direct and saves you 16 kilometres (10 miles) of walking. Locals from Ammarnäs pointed out the shorter alternative to us and, like most other hikers, we chose to take this option to save us some time. The trail is well-trodden and marked with stone cairns and seems to have become an 'unofficial' re-routing of the Kungsleden here. Where this other trail intersects with the Kungsleden proper, there is a trail junction sign indicating distances in kilometres to Ammarnäs, Adolfström, and the Rävfallet river, with two Kungsleden signs pointing south and north, so you know you are back on the right track.

Similarly, we found a discrepancy with signage from Adolfström that said Jäkkvik was a distance of 27 kilometres (16.7 miles). However, by our own reckoning after taking calculations from our map, it looked to be 21 kilometres (13 miles). Thankfully, we were correct as our tracking data indicated we had in fact walked 21.7 kilometres (13.5 miles) between the two places.

We used the Swedish 1:100,000 maps produced by Calazo and ordered them online for international delivery as we wanted them for our initial planning. They can, however, be bought in any well-equipped sports/outdoor gear store all over Sweden and are also available at the mountain stations (Hemavan, Kvikkjokk, Saltoluokta, Kebnekaise, and Abisko).

If you follow the Kungsleden without any detours, the 1:100,000 scale maps are perfectly adequate. Since our trip, however, there are newer 1:50,000 scale maps with more detail for areas such as Kebnekaise and Sarek National Park, which is especially useful if you choose to take some side trips and need to navigate in the backcountry.

The Calazo maps are light and compact, making them ideal for long-distance hikers concerned with space and weight in their packs. The Kungsleden requires four Calazo maps: Ammarnäs to Hemavan, Kvikkjokk to Ammarnäs,

Sarek and Padjelanta, and Kebnekaisefjällen (which includes Abisko). The four maps weigh a total of 140 grams (5 ounces) and cost approximately 75 Euros. (We had to purchase our set from Germany as Sweden do not post internationally.) The maps are made of Tyvek®, which is a lightweight, flexible, water- and tear-resistant material, so it is quite possible to manage without a map case.

[**i**] Tried and tested, our maps even came in handy as a footprint to protect our tent when we had to wild camp on rough ground.

The Calazo maps are not designed specifically for the Kungsleden but cover an entire area, making it possible for you to view intersecting trails, alternate valleys with backcountry routes, as well as watercourses and dominant peaks within the area. If you have not used the Calazo maps before, it doesn't take long to become accustomed to the different features and symbols on their maps, which are very universal. Both the Kungsleden's hiking and ski routes are clearly marked and labelled, with extra information, such as distances between the STF huts given on the Sarek and Padjelanta map, which is very useful and would be a good addition to the other three maps.

Digital maps can be viewed on a modern smartphone using an appropriate 'app', which is usually provided as part of any map purchase. Calazo have their own app which was updated in October 2016 with digital scale maps corresponding to 1:50,000 of Sarek, Kebnekaise, Padjelanta, and the southern mountains. For our Kungsleden walk, we used ViewRanger, which worked perfectly for our digital mapping and mobile navigation needs. The ViewRanger Shop provides Ordnance Survey maps for all parts of the UK, as well as selected long-distance paths in Europe and the rest of the world. Map segments can be purchased ad-hoc, allowing you to cover any walk you plan to take. Once downloaded, you can access the maps on your device, even if you are in an area without a mobile data signal.

Trail Regulations

Permitted Trail Use

Whilst the majority of the time you will only see foot traffic on the Kungsleden, it is possible to cycle many parts of the trail with a robust mountain bike. The Right of Public Access, or *Allemansrätten*, also allows great freedom for cycling in Sweden. As with wild camping, you must use your discretion to judge whether or not your presence will disturb or destroy, but you are allowed access to all private roads, and it is not permitted for a landowner to put up a sign prohibiting you from cycling on the road or path.

On trails intended for hikers or fell runners, such as the Kungsleden, the common accepted practice is to cycle slowly and show consideration for other users of the paths, giving way to joggers and walkers. There are some exceptions to the freedoms afforded to the cyclist in Sweden. Local authorities may decide to introduce "No Cycling" restrictions on some paths, while inside national parks and other protected areas, cycling may be banned completely.

[i] Along the Kungsleden, you will come across reindeer fences, marked on your map as *Rengärde*. Reindeer fences generally run north-west to south-east and are used to keep the animals of different cooperatives (Sámi villages) apart. There are gates where trails cross them. Otherwise, it is OK to climb across them, as long as you do not damage them.

Snowmobiles are only allowed on designated trails. In winter, you can drive through the entire Vindelfjällen Nature Reserve from Hemavan to Ammarnäs along the Kungsleden Trail but be aware that some sections might be closed off for recreational riding due to reindeer herd migration.

Vegetation & Wildlife

Along the Kungsleden, it is forbidden to disturb wildlife, hunt wildfowl or waders, disturb reindeer, climb nest trees, or intentionally approach the nests of birds of prey or mammal dens. Additionally, live wood is also protected, so you may not fell live trees or damage vegetation (e.g., by carving in the bark). As dead trees are also extremely valuable habitats for wildlife, they must be left intact and not used for fuel. However, it is permissible to collect fallen wood, cones, twigs, and branches for your campfire.

One of the great joys of being out in the forests of Sweden is the rich carpets of flowers and berries, which cover the forest floor, and the wide variety of mushrooms available at different times of year. Looking for and gathering this forest bounty is a popular activity for Swedes and visitors alike. Along the Kungsleden, you are permitted to pick flowers, berries, and mushrooms for private use but must avoid protected species and should also use your discretion for fragile species, which may not yet be formally protected. There may be local restrictions in place if a certain species is vulnerable in that area. Protection for plants and animals is usually absolute – you are not permitted to disturb them in any way. Signage, most prominent within the national parks, usually indicates any protected species and prohibitions within that area.

Camping & Fishing

You can pitch a tent for one night almost wherever you like along the Kungsleden, except for in Abisko National Park, where you must use a designated campground. In doing so, you must show consideration for reindeer husbandry and respect private property.

As a non-Swedish citizen, you are required to have a fishing license unless fishing by hand-gathering in public waters. In all other cases, you must obtain a fishing permit. Fishing is prohibited within 100 metres (330 feet) of stationary fishing equipment and fish farms. You are permitted to fish from a private jetty on an occasional basis (though not one next to someone's house) but must give priority to the owner of the jetty if they require access for a boat, etc.

Camera Drones

If you are a keen photographer and plan on bringing a drone to capture aerial footage of your Kungsleden journey, you need to be aware of the recent change in Swedish law regarding the use of camera drones. Since our trip in August/September 2016, Sweden has been one of the first countries to enforce a stringent blanket-ban on camera drones.

In October 2016, the Supreme Administrative Court of Sweden ruled that camera drones qualify as *surveillance cameras* and, therefore, require a permit under Sweden's camera surveillance laws. An application for a permit comes with a hefty fee and no guarantee of it being granted by County Administrators, who decide whether the use of your drone camera provides a legitimate benefit that outweighs public privacy. If you want one less thing to be concerned about on your trip, it is advisable that you leave your camera drone at home.

[i] As with many other aspects of the Swedish Right of Public Access, national parks and protected areas may have their own restrictions. Check online beforehand or read information boards as you enter national parks and nature reserves for current regulations.

b. Points of Interest

There are few places on earth that have the power to make you feel like you are on another planet. A mere 200 kilometres north of the Arctic Circle, among the highest peaks of Swedish Lapland, the Kungsleden is one such place. In the summertime, the sun does not set for days on end, and the terrain varies from Arctic tundra to fields of green that span as far as the eye can see.

Sámi Culture: Along with their reindeer herds, the land is home to the Sámi people, the only indigenous people in Europe, all of whom migrated thousands of years ago, from Sweden, Norway, Russia, and Finland. Take a half day to visit a Sámi camp or settlement along the route and eat typical Sámi dishes made with reindeer and elk meat as well as with fish from the local lakes and rivers. Many tour guides in the northern Kungsleden area are Sámi people who will be happy to tell you about their ancestors and the life of a reindeer breeder. The Sámi community at Tjåhke, just a short detour off the Kungsleden north of Lake Sitojaure, is a good place to learn about their ancient traditions and discover more of the Sámi culture. From Tjåhke, it is also possible to take a boat tour west along Lake Sitojaure to Rinim, a Sámi camp situated at the northwest corner of the lake.

Norra Sytertoppen: If you begin the trail from Hemavan, Norra Sytertoppen (1,768m/5,800 ft.) is an easy traverse, so hikers often take this side path as an alternate route between the STF mountain huts of Viter and Syter to summit a peak along the way and to enjoy the view of Syterskalet valley from up high.

Ammarnäs: Ammarnäs is a tiny mountain village with a population of around 280. Set in a wide river valley at the foot of the Ammarfjället mountains and by the side of the Gautsträsk lake, it is the first settlement that you will reach on the Kungsleden after leaving Hemavan. One third of the villagers here are reindeer  herders, the local Sámi people having migrated with their animals to the surrounding fells for hundreds of years.

Potato Hill: Ammarnäs has several points of interest and cultural attractions, the most famous of which is the *Potatisbacken,* or Potato Hill. Potato Hill was cultivated for the first time in the mid-1800s by one of the village's first settlers, Nils Johansson, who discovered that potatoes do not freeze as easily on the slopes of

the moraine hill. The reason being, the hill's south-facing slope, and its ability to store heat, provides a favourable climate and lengthens the growing season. It remains in full use to this day and has become a well-known point of interest throughout the country. A tractor is used to plough the hill during spring, but during the rest of the growing season, work is done by hand. There is a path leading up the back of the hill, on the top of which there is a barbecue site and a fabulous observation point. On a clear day, you will have a magnificent view of the meadows of the Ammarnäs delta and see into the southern part of Europe's largest nature reserve, the Vindelfjällen.

Sámi Church Town: On your way to the Potato Hill, you will also see that Ammarnäs has a very distinctive looking church, designed by architect Torben Grut, who also designed the Olympic Stadium in Stockholm. The first Sámi chapel of Ammarnäs was inaugurated in 1858 but was replaced in 1912 by the present church, which is

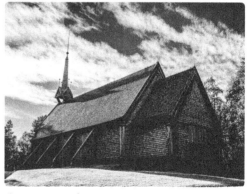

in the national romantic style and consists of a nave with a vestry to the east and a small tower above the west gable. Located close to the church are a dozen or so wooden stilted huts, which form the Sámi Church Town. These huts, perched on horizontal logs to help keep them dry, were used overnight by the Sámis when they came to worship at the church. Today, the church town is still in use as Sámi families continue to gather here three times a year to celebrate important festivals, and the huts are now considered some of the best-preserved church buildings in Västerbotten.

Kvikkjokk: If your itinerary allows, Kvikkjokk makes for a good 'zero' hiking day as the Tarra river and Kamajåkkå stream join here, so you might like the opportunity to rent a canoe or take a boat trip up the Tarra river delta.

Mount Skierfe: For the Sámi people, the mountains often had religious connotations and several were *Sieidi* (places of worship). Offerings, such as antlers from reindeer, were regularly made in such places. One of the most significant Sieidi was situated at the foot of Mount Skierfe at the entrance to the Rapa valley, where Sámis from the entire region gathered for special ceremonies. Not only does this mountain have historical significance, but from the flat summit, you will see possibly one of the best views in Sweden! Therefore, the lookout point atop of Skierfe (1,179m/3,868 ft.), reached by taking a 8-kilometre (5 miles) detour off the Kungsleden, is something not to be missed. Situated on the eastern border of Sarek National Park, the long, deep, narrow valleys and the wild, turbulent, grey-green colour waters caused by the sediment create a fantastic delta landscape in the Rapadalen valley, some 600 metres below. In good weather, this incredible vista presents a perfect photo opportunity. If you want to take a closer look at the delta, from Aktse it is possible to take boat transportation through the delta of Rapaätno to the Rapa valley, where you can explore a little more of Sarek.

Leavas Sámi Village: Leavas Sámi village has a summer camp close to Alesjaure. Socially structured, a Sámi village, or *siida*, is a reindeer foraging area, a group for reindeer herding, and a cooperative working for the economic benefit of its members all in one. If you visit here at the beginning of July, there is a good chance to participate in the Sámi calf marking. Although a considerable number of Sámi now live in Stockholm and work office hours, the traditional culture and language continues, and crafts like knife-making, bone and antler engraving, woodcarving, and tin-wire embroidery remain an important source of income. If your transport connections take you through Jokkmokk, there is an interesting Sámi museum, Ájtte (meaning Storehouse), if you want to find out more. The waterfall on the east side of Alesjaure is also worth a day tour. The hiking extends past the Sámi village and onward several kilometres.

Mount Njullá: If you are hiking the Kungsleden south to north, on the final segment of your journey, you will be walking through the verdant Abisko valley. Here, the beautiful and easily accessible Mount Njullá (1,164m/3,820 ft.), known for its profusion of flowers, makes a good side trip, especially as there is a chair lift to take you

up the mountain all year round. As the highest peak in Abisko National Park, from the summit, you are afforded a magnificent view of Torneträsk lake and if you look to the west, it is possible to see the snow-capped mountains of Norway. The Abiskojåkka river flows through the long valley and close to the Tourist Station and Naturum Visitor Centre, rushing forward through a beautiful limestone canyon. Several other trails and nature paths also traverse Abisko National Park, which you may want to explore if you have some days to spare after finishing the Kungsleden.

National Parks: Sweden was the first country in Europe to establish the national park concept in 1909. Traversing 5 of Sweden's 29 national parks along the 430-kilometre route, the Kungsleden comprises a magnificent mosaic of different landscape types, from the leafy birch forests and alpine peaks of Stora Sjöfallet, to Padjelanta's

sparkling fresh water lakes and vast expanses of open moorland. The entire Kungsleden is a vast wilderness adventure, but the national parks are some of the route's main highlights. Whether your intention is to hike just a section of the Kungsleden or complete the entire trail, side trips and/or extra days can easily by spent exploring the national parks further. The best of which are described in the side trips section of the appendix.

Swedish Sauna: Finally, an experience you certainly should not miss along the Kungsleden is relaxing in a traditional wood-fired Swedish sauna. After a long day in the mountains, the warmth of a wood-heated sauna and the cold of a dip in a nearby stream or lake make for a wonderful combination.

Saunas are available at many STF huts and mountain stations along the Kungsleden route. So if you have already paid to use the facilities, make sure you indulge in a sauna at least once on your trip. For us, it was a wonderful new experience on a thru-hike and a great insight into Swedish culture.

c. Weather

This book is about the summer hiking season, which, in northern Sweden, is typically late June until late September, when the STF mountain huts along the trail are open and manned. Although the Kungsleden is mostly frequented during summer, it remains open in winter, typically mid-February until late April/early May, when it becomes a ski trail.

[!] Depending on your experience and level of expertise, it is recommended that you use a tour company or guide during the winter period, as hiking requires much more knowledge and specialised equipment, not covered in this guide.

Each part of summer has its own characteristics, but as the Arctic is so unpredictable, the trail can always be susceptible to rain and severe mountain weather, whichever month you choose. Some years have encountered better conditions than others (i.e., sunnier and warmer climes). If you start your hike at the beginning of the season in June, the Tjäktja Pass (highest point of the Kungsleden) will still most likely be covered in snow, so think carefully about your footwear and prepare for this. As the summer thaw increases, the rivers flow fast and full. However, this should not impact on your progress, as all major crossings on the trail have bridges.

Rain is common in the summer and even snow can occur. Being in a subarctic climate, it can also be bitterly cold. From late August, it is common to have temperatures below freezing at night. It might be that winter may arrive early, so be mindful of snowfall in September before the end of the season, as this creates a muddier trail and makes river crossings more difficult.

Rowing boats are usually in place by late June/early July, but, similarly, lake crossings can be hampered by severe weather. If you are planning on hiking the entire trail, make sure you leave yourself enough time to cross the last lakes before the rowing boats are removed for winter. This generally means completing the trail by mid-September, but the closing dates differ slightly from year to year. (Check the STF website for exact dates.)

In northern Sweden, above the Arctic Circle, the Midnight Sun is visible 24 hours a day between 27th May and 18th July. If you want to witness this and have infinite daylight for long hiking days, then you should plan to start your hike early July. Yet keep in mind, you may find it difficult to sleep with the sun shining on your tent at 2:00 AM! Another benefit of starting early summer is that biting insects, such as mosquitoes, will be less problematic.

High season is classed as mid-July to late August when summer fully arrives in the Swedish mountains. Sunshine and blue skies are never guaranteed, but any lingering snow should be gone from the trail, and it is likelier that the weather will be more favourable. However, if you want to avoid the horrors of the mosquitoes, which are fervently active at this time, then the walking season is short – just mid-August to mid-September. (Even then you may still not be able to avoid them completely!)

[ⓘ] In Sweden, mid-August is the time when the new school year starts, so this is generally a point after which less Swedish hikers find their way up the Kungsleden. The trail will almost certainly be quietest around mid-September, when the huts begin to empty and close for the season.

Temperature

In a land as varied as Sweden, seasons can be quite different depending on where you live. The country's climate is influenced by the Gulf Stream, a warm ocean stream that flows off Norway's west coast. For simplicity's sake, the country can be divided into three major regions: Götaland in the south, Svealand in the middle, and Norrland in the north. The temperatures discussed here are for northern Sweden as this is the part of the country that the Kungsleden traverses.

Summers may be short, but temperatures are often a comfortable 15°C (60°F), which is perfect for walking, with occasional peaks of up to 30°C (86°F). Sweden is located in the Central European Time (CET) zone. Like in other European countries, *Summer Time* is also observed here. This means that the clock is set forward one hour, from the last weekend in March to the last weekend in October, for the purpose of gaining more daylight.

On the other hand, winters in northern Sweden are long, cold, and dry, with below-freezing temperatures lasting several months. There is also much more snow in the north. This typically means that before mid-June, the Kungsleden is not normally passable with boots – you either need skis or snowshoes. In midwinter, there is no daylight at all north of the Arctic Circle. Instead, you might be lucky enough to experience the sky lit up by the Northern Lights, but this is never guaranteed.

The table below shows average annual temperatures for three significant locations along the Kungsleden. To estimate the temperatures along the trail, it is helpful to use a lapse rate. As a rule of thumb, deduct 3°C for every 300 metres (1,000 feet) in elevation gain from the respective temperature of your hiking month.

Month	Hemavan (484m ASL)		Kvikkjokk (334m ASL)		Abisko (408m ASL)	
	Max (°C)	Min (°C)	Max (°C)	Min (°C)	Max (°C)	Min (°C)
January	-4	-10	-4	-11	-4	-10
February	-4	-10	-4	-11	-4	-10
March	-2	-7	-1	-8	-2	-7
April	1	-4	2	-4	1	-4
May	7	1	8	2	5	1
June	14	7	15	8	13	7
July	17	9	18	11	17	10
August	15	8	16	9	15	9
September	10	4	11	5	10	4
October	4	0	4	0	3	0
November	-1	-5	-1	-5	-1	-5
December	-3	-9	-3	-9	-3	-9

Source: Metroblue.com, Period 1985-2014.

Table 2 – Average Temperatures along Kungsleden

Starting the trail in Hemavan in July, expect minimum daily temperatures of around 9°C (48°F), with the maximum daily temperature typically around 17°C (63°F). Kvikkjokk can be considered as roughly the halfway point on the Kungsleden. As it is 150 metres (500 feet) lower in elevation than Hemavan, you can expect average temperatures to be a degree or so warmer here. Reaching the end of the trail in Abisko, temperatures will not be too different to those experienced at the start of your trip. However, as the lengthening nights of September arrive, you can find that the temperatures along the trail may drop unexpectedly as the weather becomes more unsettled.

[!] Remember, it can snow at any time, and you can actually be snowed in if the weather turns and temperature drops significantly. By the end of September, it is common to have below-freezing temperatures at night.

Although the Kungsleden is crisscrossed with vast lakes and numerous streams that look extremely inviting, consider that the water temperature may feel as arctic as your location. If you're not used to swimming in cold water, think about your safety. Shivering and teeth chattering are the first symptoms of hypothermia. If that happens, get out of the water immediately. Take warm clothes to put on after your swim as, even in summer, you'll feel colder when you get out.

[i] Try to coincide any lake swims with STF huts that have sauna facilities, as you can return to the sauna to quickly increase your body temperature after exposing yourself to extremely cold water.

Precipitation

The table below shows the average annual precipitation for the same three locations along the Kungsleden.

Month	Hemavan (484m ASL)		Kvikkjokk (334m ASL)		Abisko (408m ASL)	
	Rain (mm)	Average Rainfall (days)	Rain (mm)	Average Rainfall (days)	Rain (mm)	Average Rainfall (days)
Jan	74	18	47	17	90	19
Feb	62	17	45	15	75	18
Mar	62	18	50	17	81	20
Apr	48	16	49	16	62	19
May	55	16	65	17	73	20
Jun	71	15	88	16	111	20
Jul	94	17	122	18	165	22
Aug	88	16	97	17	122	20
Sep	80	18	85	17	100	21
Oct	77	19	70	18	98	21
Nov	64	17	55	17	71	19
Dec	73	20	51	17	90	20
Annual	848	207	824	202	1138	239

Source: Metroblue.com, Period 1985-2014.

Table 3 – Average Precipitation along Kungsleden

You can see from the table that the most popular months on the Kungsleden are also some of the wettest. For each of the months July, August, and September, it is expected to rain for at least half the amount of days. This can range from persistent light showers to brief downpours of heavy rain between valleys.

Taking all of the above information into account, our best piece of advice is to be prepared for rain at any time. The amount of rain can vary, but you would be very unlucky to find yourself in persistent heavy rainfall over several days. As clouds start to form, it is good to organise your gear so that your rain jacket and waterproof trousers are readily available either in your front pouch or at the top of your pack. Your waterproof pack cover should also be easily accessible should the need arise to use it.

[!] It is important to remember that when seeking shelter during a thunderstorm, move away from freestanding trees and place your pack and other metal objects at a distance. Avoid peaks and passes and stay low to the ground among scattered boulders or trees.

As the impending weather is usually everyone's greatest concern, most of the STF huts and private accommodation along the way will have the latest forecasts and information regarding the current weather and conditions, although this is extremely changeable between valleys that seem to have their own unique micro-climate whatever the forecast. The Swedish Meteorological and Hydrological Institute website (*www.smhi.se/en*) is also a good place to find the latest updates for your location if you have access to the internet.

d. Camping

This section covers the basics of camping along the Kungsleden. Included are the various rules and regulations you must follow in choosing and using wild campsites. Allemansrätten, or Everyone's Right, provides a unique freedom of access to Sweden's countryside and wild places, allowing you to camp virtually anywhere, provided you follow a few simple rules and the leave no trace ethic. This means leaving the land exactly as you found it, with no evidence of you ever having been there.

Alternatively, there are several established campsites along the route located beside water sources and close to the STF mountain huts, which allow campers the use of their facilities, including toilets and indoor cooking areas. To camp at these locations and use the facilities provided, you must pay a fee set each year by the Swedish Tourist Association. A list of STF accommodation with distances and elevation figures, where camping is also available on-site, is included in Section 3d *Trail Shelters*.

General Rules

Sweden is filled with forests and open landscapes and one of the unique joys of living in Sweden is *Allemansrätten*, the Right of Public Access. It allows anyone to roam freely in the countryside, swim, and travel by boat in someone else's waters and pick mushrooms and berries in the forest. Although landowners can put up signs to exclude visitors from certain private lands and areas that are particularly vulnerable to damage are always off-limits, the general rule is that visitors can walk across lands at a reasonable distance from houses, yards, gardens, and fenced-in areas. With this right comes the responsibility to tread carefully and to show consideration for landowners and others. Except for the area nearest a person's house, you even have the right to camp or park a motor home on another person's land for up to 24 hours. After this time, you will need the landowner's permission to stay.

Generally, a good rule of thumb is to ensure that you pitch your tent out of sight of people's houses and do not stay more than two nights in the same spot. Don't forget to take all of your litter away with you (including food scraps – orange peel, for example, can take many years to degrade naturally). If no other option exists, make sure you bury your toilet waste properly. Choose a spot at least 50 metres (165 feet) from houses, camping spots, water sources, etc. Dig a hole 15 centimetres (6 inches) deep for your waste and then fill in soil on top. Do not bury non-degradable items, such as female sanitary products. Pack them out and dispose of them at the next available trash bin, typically provided alongside toilet facilities at Fjällstations and hostels.

Most areas of Sweden have very good facilities for recycling. In addition to the standard containers for glass, paper, and cans common in the UK, many small towns or village supermarkets will also have stations to recycle batteries and plastics. You will also find this is the case on the Kungsleden, whereby the STF huts have a strict recycling policy that you must adhere to when using their facilities. You must clean, sort, and separate your rubbish and put it in the appropriate containers provided by each hut along the trail.

Campfires

With regards to campfires, lighting fires is permitted under the Right of Public Access, but you must follow certain precautions to minimise damage and the risk of an uncontrolled fire. Many people do not think of Sweden as a hot country, but, in fact, during the summer, the forests and heathlands can become extremely dry, and large forest fires are a very real danger. Therefore, you must site your fire where there is no risk of it spreading and where the fire will not cause damage. A good place is on sandy ground or gravel. Avoid mossy and peat-bog areas, as the fire is likely to spread and can also smoulder unnoticed in the ground, then flare up again long after you have left. Additionally, you should not light your fire next to a rock, as this can crack and scar the rock. Wet stones may crack and even explode when heated.

You are permitted to gather fallen cones, twigs, and branches for your fire. But you must not cut down trees or shrubs or remove twigs, branches, or bark from living trees. Also, fallen trees must not be used for fuel. Dead trees are extremely valuable habitats for wildlife and must be left intact.

At times where there is a high risk of fire, a ban may be imposed by the local authority. In this case, you are not allowed to light fires but may still use designated grill spots and a camping stove with care. National parks and nature reserves in Sweden may have their own regulations regarding campfires. You will find the rules posted in English on noticeboards around the area. You can also make enquiries with the local municipality or county administrative board about the current fire risk level, which often provide a recorded message service. Numbers can be found under *Brandförsvar* (fire protection) or *Räddningstjänst* (rescue service).

Established Campsites

As wild camping is permitted along the entire Kungsleden route – apart from Abisko National Park, where it is restricted to designated campgrounds only – you should not find any real difficulty with locating a suitable place to camp. Water is plentiful along the route, and it is almost a certainty that whenever you cross a flowing water source, you will find an established campsite located just off the trail.

This is particularly evident in the northernmost section where you will pass numerous previously established camp spots complete with fire rings made out of rocks and/or seats made out of logs, the ingenuity of hikers creating some extra comforts benefitting the next passer-by. This doesn't really follow the principles of the 'Leave no Trace' ethic, but what it does is encourage hikers to use existing sites instead of creating new camp spots, thereby potentially damaging more vegetation.

The terrain and condition of the ground as well as whether a location is open to the elements will be your prime concern when choosing where to pitch your tent. This can be troublesome if you find yourself traversing a particularly boggy or rocky section of the trail. But as mountain huts are not typically too far apart, you will always have the option of camping next to a hut, where you are guaranteed to find a maintained area specifically designated for camping, usually with much better ground conditions.

On sections of the trail with heavier foot traffic, for your convenience, you will even find the presence of pit toilets, so as to keep toileting in the wild to a minimum and the trail clear of litter.

Figure 15 – Typical Established Campsite | Typical Pit Toilet along the Route

Choosing a Wild Camping Site

If you find yourself camping in between mountain huts or if you plan on taking off-trail side trips, consider the following factors when choosing a campsite:

Strategy – Pick campsites that are convenient milestones for the distance and difficulty of each trail section. You will find that the existing campsites are often ideally located in this regard. Many are located just before more difficult sections of the trail, enabling you to tackle the most challenging portion of your day early on, while your legs are fresh and before temperatures begin to rise.

Comfort – Avoid camping in basins and dips, where cold air will gather, and in close proximity to water. Moisture and dew can attract mosquitos, soak your gear, or cover it in frost. Moving just a few steps up and away from these areas can make for a much more comfortable night. At the same time, you want to have reasonably easy access to water for washing and cooking. Ideally, your campsite will also provide wind shelter while allowing the sun to shine brightly from the east to warm and dry your tent and sleeping bag in the morning. Choose dry sand or small gravel over any organic substance and vegetation to prevent moisture from creeping into your tent through the floor.

Safety – Do not camp under or around dead trees! Falling trees and limbs can be a safety hazard and should not be underestimated, especially during windy conditions. Make sure to always check overhead first before choosing a campsite in the woods.

Impact on Nature – Minimising your environmental impact helps preserve the trail and surrounding areas for fellow hikers and future generations. Here are a few basic principles you should follow when choosing a campsite (courtesy of the Leave No Trace Centre for Outdoor Ethics):

- Camp on durable surfaces such as rock, gravel, sand, or snow. Avoid any type of vegetation if possible. At higher altitudes, it is more sensitive and may never recover.

- Camp at previously established sites or places that are suitable for camping as-is, i.e., you don't have to move rocks, branches, etc.

- Keep your campsite as small as possible to minimise disturbance.

- Camp at least 60 metres (200 feet) from lakes and streams.

e. Water

Throughout the Kungsleden, access to water should not be problematic. The trail crosses numerous watercourses each day, with a couple of hours walk typically being the longest stretch before finding a flowing source where you can fill up your supplies. As you will be passing through uninhabited areas for the majority of your time, water can be taken directly from rivers and streams and safely drank without the need to purify it. Advice given from the Swedish Tourist Association is that as long as the water is flowing, it is safe to drink[1]. It is so pristine and clear, you can drink it straight from the source.

This is a particularly wonderful element of the Kungsleden trail as being able to fill up water supplies regularly means you can carry less. Furthermore, it also saves you a lot of time, as filling up and purifying several litres of water a few times each day can be a very time-consuming process.

---

1   https://www.swedishtouristassociation.com/faq/is-it-safe-to-drink-the-water-from-mountain-streams/

This is very different to other long-distance hikes you may have completed, whereby the advice given is to always filter and treat any water coming from natural sources prior to consumption. Even though you do not have to do this along the Kungsleden, for best practice, the subject of water purification is discussed further in Section 5d *Food & Water*.

Figure 16 – Refilling Water straight from Flowing Stream | Trail Humour

At accommodation along the trail, it is only the Fjällstations that have hot, running water. Most STF huts do not have water piped to the cabins, although some huts, such as Aktse and Alesjaure, are beginning to develop easier on-site water systems. Instead, hikers are responsible for topping up supplies by collecting fresh water from a nearby river or lake (used for drinking, cooking, and washing), denoted with a sign saying *Vatten* (drinking water). There is usually a large wooden container to discard used water from the kitchen, known as the *slask* (waste water).

Downstream from the drinking water is where you can do any necessary washing, denoted with a sign saying *Tvatt* (washing). Where huts have sauna facilities, there is usually an adjoining washroom. But again, you have to collect water from the river or lake for washing. However, you can heat it first using the water jacket around the sauna stove.

[!] In order to avoid contamination of natural water sources, if you are not using the facilities provided by the huts, keep at least a distance of 30 metres (100 feet) when washing yourself, your clothing, or cooking utensils. Use bio-degradable soap or, ideally, refrain from using any kind of detergent altogether. Furthermore, leftover food and human waste should be buried at least 30 centimetres (12 inches) deep and 60 metres (200 feet) away from water sources. Fortunately, as there are so many toilets provided along the Kungsleden, it would be a rare occurrence to go in the bush.

f. Flora & Fauna

The Kungsleden will bring you face to face with some truly stunning features of the natural world – far more than this book is able to cover. This section is intended to provide an overview of the most prominent plants and animals. If you are interested in a more in-depth view of the Kungsleden's flora and fauna, recommendations for additional reading are provided in the *Links & References* section of the appendix.

Vegetation

Trailing over heather-covered moors, through dense birch forests to fells covered in wild flowers, the Kungsleden showcases a range of lush and dense vegetation despite its harsh mountain climate. In lakeside marshes and along rivers, it is common to spot spear thistles with their vibrant purple petals attracting bees and wasps. Also attracting insects and butterflies during the summer, golden yellow buttercups carpet large open areas at lower elevations. Other common plants you will encounter on the Kungsleden are described below:

Blueberry

17% of Sweden is said to be covered in *blåbär* (bilberries and wild blueberries), so they inevitably play a prominent part in Swedish cuisine. They grow wild on small bushes close to the ground and are found in abundance along the Kungsleden route. Enjoys handfuls of fresh blueberries as you walk! They are a great source of vitamins and have huge health benefits on a trail where it is otherwise difficult to obtain fresh food.

Figure 17 – Wild Blueberries | Enjoying a Handful

Bog Cotton

The Arctic cottongrass or 'bog cotton' is the most widespread flowering plant found in the northern hemisphere and Arctic tundra regions. It looks very much like cotton wool blowing in the wind, but, in fact, the 'hairs' are modified petals and sepals that, with the assistance of the wind, provide long-distance dispersal of the attached seeds. Spotting those fluffy white heads alongside the trail is a sure sign of boggy, wet ground, to be avoided completely when looking for a wild camp spot. But use this to your advantage, as boggy ground is also the best spot for locating cloudberries – Sweden's national symbol and prized treasure.

Cloudberry

This yellow/orange distinctive fruit grows wild in the mountains of northern Sweden. It is extremely difficult to cultivate, as it needs acidic soil on high boggy ground. So if you want to sample one, look out for cloudberries along the Kungsleden in water-logged areas. The cloudberry is extremely hardy but the season is short. Usually, they are all gone by mid-August. The plants begin to flower in June and the berries usually ripen in July, each stem boasting just a single berry. At first, the berries are red, but as they ripen, they turn a beautiful golden yellow.

Figure 18 – Bog Cotton alongside the Trail | A Special Treat: Cloudberry

Mushrooms

There are several hundreds of different species of mushrooms and fungi. Many of them are delicious, others are deadly, so beware if you decide to pick them to spice up your trail food. Karljohan is one of the most common and edible mushrooms, appearing in small clusters all over Sweden with pine, spruce, or several other trees. It is compact and surprisingly heavy, with big specimens weighing close to a kilogram (2 pounds). Many animals and insects, particularly snails, love karljohan, so it's quite common for something to have already nibbled on your find. Generally, you will have to walk further from the trail to find anything substantial, as mushrooms within easy reach will have already been picked. Another popular mushroom variety is the kantarell or golden chanterelle. It is considered by many chefs to be equal to the truffle and is a prized find along the Kungsleden from July to September.

Figure 19 – Large Karljohan Mushroom | Beware of Poisonous Species

Birch

Found in the mountainous regions of Sweden and so a prominent feature of the Kungsleden, the silver birch is a medium-sized deciduous tree that owes its common name to the white peeling bark on the trunk. On the trail, dry birch bark is good for getting your campfire started, and the sap produces a delicious aroma that seems to keep mosquitoes at bay. The tree supports a wide range of insects, and many species of birds and animals are found in birch woodland. The light shade it casts allows shrubby and other plants to grow beneath its canopy. The Ornäs birch is a variety of silver birch with deeply indented leaves that is the national tree of Sweden.

The mountains are a rough and exposed environment for any growing life. An important factor for mountain flora is altitude and proximity to the north. Yet, as the climate of the mountainous regions is relatively stable, the plants have been able to adapt over time to the harsh conditions. You will notice many mountain plants are smaller in size, and it's common that they create alternative growth patterns, like bows, carpets, and tussocks, in order to protect themselves from wind and frost. The change in season between summer and autumn brings a change of colour and so is one of the best times to see the flora on the Kungsleden in all its glory.

Wildlife

The vast and seemingly unending forests and lakes along the Kungsleden provide habitats for a variety of species. These hardy species are equipped with the capacity to survive the intensity of the seasons in Sweden, making them unique animals indeed. The following species have been highlighted due to their abundance, visibility, and/or uniqueness to Sweden, but elusive as they are, whether you will be lucky enough to see them along the trail, who can say?

Reindeer

The exception to this is reindeer, as it is possible to see them almost all year round, particularly in the summer, where they spend their time grazing on the higher fells along the Kungsleden route. Reindeer in Sweden today are semi-domesticated. Wild reindeer having been extinct since the 1800s. The Sámi are the sole owners of the reindeer, meaning they are the only ones that can herd and hunt them. Sighting other mammals along the trail, however, is much more difficult.

Figure 20 – Reindeer near Lake Alesjaure | Crossing a Reindeer Fence

Moose

The moose, commonly considered the 'King of the Swedish Forest', is the largest deer animal in the world, measuring two metres (6'7") in height and weighing up to 400-500 kilograms (880-1100 pounds). Sweden has a very large moose population, around 250,000, with about 100,000 moose shot during hunting every year. Its pelt is a shaggy grey/brown and its legs are pale grey. The bull begins to develop antlers in its first year. The antlers become larger each year until the age of 6-9 years. Moose hoof-prints are large and pointed. However, sighting a moose along the trail is much rarer than what you would expect. Apart from taking a guided wildlife watching tour, the best place to see moose along the Kungsleden is from Kaitumjaure, where there is a resident moose often seen wandering in the lakeside marches.

Carnivores

Carnivores, such as brown bear, wolverine, and lynx, are known to roam the wilds of northern Sweden. However, being such solitary and nocturnal creatures, sightings are not common, particularly during the busy summer season on the trail. Winter offers a better opportunity, as it may be possible to spot tracks in the snow, which may lead to a rare sighting of one of the big three. (Although still highly unlikely.)

Lemmings

The lemming is an endemic species of Scandinavia and a frequent sighting on the Kungsleden. They are small, short-tailed, thickset rodents related to voles and found in the Arctic tundra. They are the main prey of the Arctic fox. Lemmings typically graze on mosses and sedges but sometimes become a pest by chewing through tents and gear if left unattended. During some years, the species can have enormous population growth. For example, one female can give birth to as much as 13 pups each month. The years after a lemming peak, the population crashes almost down to zero. In 2016, we didn't see a single lemming on the trail from start to finish.

Forest Birds

Aside from reindeer, forest birds are the most common wildlife you'll encounter on the Kungsleden. Redpolls, willow warblers, blue throats, and bramblings are typical in the birch forest, whereas golden plovers and dotterels can be spotted in the alpine heaths. The black grouse, common in Norrland's forests, are hunted in the autumn for their feathers and unique taste. The willow grouse lives in both coniferous and mountain birch forest and can be identified by its summer plumage, which is more reddish-brown than the ptarmigan's, and its larger body and beak. Above the treeline, the dotterel breeds from June to mid-August and is usually spotted on high plateaus with short vegetation. Its summer plumage comprises a characteristic rust-brown breast with a white breast-band. You might also be fortunate to spot a bird of prey. Along the Kungsleden, golden eagles, white-tailed eagles, rough-legged buzzards, and gyr falcons can sometimes be seen hunting in the sky.

Fish

In a country with almost 100,000 lakes with crystal clear waters, you are bound to see grayling, Arctic char, or maybe even trout on your journey along the Kungsleden. Most common at higher altitudes, Arctic char can grow up to 75 centimetres (30 inches) in length and can weigh up to 7 kilograms (15 pounds). It needs oxygen-rich water and feeds on small crustaceans, insects, and other fish. The Arctic char is easy to spot, as the bright tips of its fins can be seen from afar in the water. Remember, if you intend on fishing in lakes and waterways that you pass on the Kungsleden, you will need a fishing permit. These are usually available to purchase from a tourist office, campsite, or local shop. A typical one-day pass is around 70 SEK (£6.50), with a week's pass offering a small discount and giving better value at around 220 SEK (£20). However, prices can vary according to specific areas.

g. Safety

Hiking is multidimensional. It offers something for your mind and your body. If you hike along the Kungsleden in northernmost Swedish Lapland, you will see some of the most beautiful things that Sweden has to offer. But you must always consider potential hazards and minimise risks to your safety. You are, after all, hiking in the Arctic.

General Precautions

First and foremost, it's important to make sure that someone knows your planned route and when you're expecting to be back. Tell someone who can raise the alarm if you don't return as planned.

Route & Weather

Adapt your trip according to the weather. The weather can change quickly in the mountains. Check local weather forecasts on the radio or at *www.smhi. se*. Weather services are also available as apps for mobile phones, although bear in mind in many areas along the Kungsleden, there's no mobile phone coverage. Always respect mountain weather warnings issued.

Keep to the Kungsleden route by following the marked trails. Distance markers and cairns are there for a reason. Follow the trails – this will make it easier for you to find your way, and it's safer in case you need help for any reason. Remember, red crosses indicate winter trails, which aren't always appropriate to follow in summer.

Take a map and compass with you. Make sure your map is up-to-date. The compass will mainly be needed if you divert off the marked trails, e.g., going into the backcountry to explore Sarek National Park. Know how to use your compass. Use GPS as a backup, but remember that batteries discharge quickly when cold.

Ask experienced people for advice. People who often spend time in the mountains can give you vital information, such as the hosts at the STF's mountain huts. Get in touch with them and ask questions about routes, water levels, bridges, and anything else that might make your planning easier. Local mountain safety committees know all kinds of things about their local mountains.

If conditions deteriorate so you doubt that you can attain your goal, turn back. Don't try to defy the weather, as others may risk their lives to rescue you. If you change your goal, be sure to notify whoever is expecting you.

River Crossings

Large rivers along the Kungsleden route are so well bridged that you shouldn't encounter any dangerous crossings. But if you do have to ford smaller rivers or streams, choose your crossing point wisely. Always take care and exercise caution, as rocks can be slippery and unstable. When crossing, use your walking poles or a stick for extra balance to avoid falling over and as a probe to read the river bottom.

Figure 21 – Makeshift Bridge across Stream | Typical Wooden Bridge across River

[i] Some people carry sandals specifically for river crossings to keep their hiking footwear dry. Make sure sandals have a strap and a sole with good grip.

Emergency Assistance

Sweden has a rescue service, but you may have to pay for it if you have been negligent or irresponsible. Many huts have shortwave emergency radios (they are marked by a phone symbol on maps) but off the trail, caution (and company) is advisable. A broken ankle can mean a long crawl to the nearest hut. Remember, the place is not regularly patrolled in the way, for instance, the U.S. National Parks are. In Sweden, out in the wilderness you are generally on your own. If possible, call 112 in an emergency or use an emergency phone in a nearby mountain shelter

Additionally, you may wish to carry a satellite communicator. There are several types of portable, electronic communication devices available, the basic model providing a personal locator beacon for one-way emergency communication. This will give location information when the operator sends a distress message. An SOS signal coming from a locator beacon is recognised by Search and Rescue as a true emergency, and they will usually act immediately.

Flora & Fauna

When it comes to nature in Sweden, there is so much of it, but essentially you will not find anything to be dangerous, unless you are allergic or hypersensitive. Wasps actually kill more people than any other animal in Sweden, but it is only about one per year. A bite from the most poisonous spider in Sweden is about as harmful to humans as a mosquito bite and the only poisonous snake, the adder(or viper), is also fairly harmless, unless you happen to be allergic. Of the top fifty most dangerous snakes in the world, zero can be found in Sweden.

Mosquitoes

A bothersome insect you will almost certainly come across at some point on the Kungsleden is the mosquito (*mygg*). They generally appear around mid-June and disappear again towards the end of September, with numbers lowest at the beginning and end of the season. Since mosquitoes like water and birch forest, they are not often found on the high plains above the treeline. Sweden has 47 species of mosquito, 45 of which are the biting kind, though not all of these will bite humans. Only female mosquitoes bite humans, as they require the protein to breed. While mosquitoes can be a serious nuisance on the trail, in Sweden, these insects are disease free and mostly harmless.

Generally, mosquitoes in Sweden are only a particular problem during dusk hours and are prevalent more in the north of the country than elsewhere. Protect yourself from attack by using a repellent that includes DEET. If you are prone to bites and find them particularly irritating, it is a good idea to carry a mosquito head net in your pack. Also wearing insect repellent clothing, such as trousers and long-sleeved shirts/tops that are bite-proof, can make you more comfortable and less of a target.

Ticks

Ticks (*fästingar*) are something to be aware of, as they are more dangerous than they might at first seem. As carriers of Lyme disease and tick-borne encephalitis (TBE), they have become a serious pest to hikers. Lyme disease, a viral infectious disease involving the central nervous system, is difficult to diagnose, so may be undetected. Early symptoms can include fever, headache, fatigue, and a skin rash. It is treatable with antibiotics if it's diagnosed early. But neurological problems and joint pain can develop months or years later if Lyme disease is left untreated. In the worst cases, it can be fatal.

The best way for walkers to avoid getting bitten is to use repellent and wear light coloured clothes, so that ticks can easily be seen. Walk on paths, avoiding long grass or verges, where possible. If you need to remove a tick, use fine tipped tweezers or a tick-removal tool to grasp the tick by the head as close to the skin as possible. Pull firmly and steadily, without twisting, as this could increase the risk of infection by prompting the tick to regurgitate saliva into the bite wound. After the tick is removed, apply antiseptic and beware of a rash. (We recommend that it is worth purchasing a tick-removal tool and keeping it in your first aid kit.)

Bears

The brown bear is Sweden's biggest and perhaps most ferocious beast. Size, body weight, and colour vary between species, geographic location, and general food availability. The largest bears, the "Big Browns", exist along the coast of Alaska and Russia, growing to very large sizes, rivalling that of the Polar Bear, whereas the interior bears of the North American Rocky Mountains (Grizzly Bear) and the mountains of Europe tend to be much smaller. The European brown bear stands 1.70 to 2.20 metres (5'6" to 7'2") tall and depending on the distribution region, its weight can vary between 100 and 350 kilograms (220-770 pounds). While attacks are extremely rare, bears ARE known to attack in Sweden, especially when freshly woken from hibernation or when they feel their young are under threat. However, the chances that you will meet a bear on the Kungsleden are so close to zero that there is absolutely no reason to fear it.

[i] Wild animals will normally avoid encounters with people. To prevent stress situations for yourself or animals, make your presence known, e.g., by talking or singing loudly. Never feed wild animals and keep your food out of reach when you camp. Take into account that animals with cubs or youngsters feel more easily threatened and can easily become aggressive.

Mushrooms

Be aware that there are killer mushrooms in Sweden! The *Toppig Spindelskivling*, otherwise known as 'deadly webcap' in English is extremely poisonous. Reddish/brown, this mushroom is an agaric, with gills and often confused with a chanterelle, which is lighter in colour. It can be recognised as having a cap that is convex instead of concave that usually has a pointed tip in the middle. Other potentially lethal mushrooms include the *Röd Flugsvamp* (red fly), distinctive by its flat red hat with white dots, the *Amanita Muscaria* (ly agaric), also characterised by a red top with white dots but with a dome shape, the *Vit Flugsvamp* or 'white fly mushroom' (known in English as the 'destroying angel'), and the *Lömsk Flugsvamp* or 'sneaky fly mushroom' (in English known as the 'death cap').

[!] As a general rule and because it is difficult to distinguish between mushrooms that are safe to eat and those that are toxic, never pick a mushroom unless you are 100% certain it is edible.

h. Other Conditions

Hunting Season

Hunting in Sweden is practically a national pastime with almost 300,000 hunters in a population of just over 9 million. The hunting season spans from August to February and is split into various periods depending on species and region. Hunting accidents with firearms are relatively rare. But you can minimise risks when hiking by wearing a blaze-orange-coloured vest, hat, or pack cover, so that you will be visible to hunters. If you don't have any of these, make sure you wear bright colours and steer clear of earth tones.

Many factors, such as the lunar calendar, affect peak times of day for animal activity and, hence, hunting. However, as a rule of thumb, these usually coincide with sunrise and sunset. Therefore, it's best to avoid being in hunting areas during these times, since you'll be less visible in the dim light. If you are on the trail at such times, use a headlamp or flashlight and wear reflective material. Talk with your companions or whistle if you're hiking alone to make your presence on the trail known. If you hear shooting, shout to notify hunters that you are there.

Holidays

Choosing to hike during either the school holiday or national holiday periods will mean an increase in traffic on the trail by way of weekend walkers or section hikers, as people head to the hills for some quality time outdoors. If you prefer solitude on the trail, carefully consider your chosen dates. There is currently a total of 14 permanent public holidays in Sweden. The majority of establishments, such as banks, shops, and restaurants, are closed on Midsummer's Day, Christmas Eve, Christmas Day, and New Year's Day. For the rest of the year, Sunday hours apply to public holidays. These include[2]:

- New Year's Day (Jan 1)
- Epiphany (Jan 6)
- Good Friday, Easter Sunday, and Easter Monday (with changeable dates based on the Christian calendar)
- International Workers' Day/Labour Day (May 1)
- Ascension Day (Changeable: 40 days after Easter)
- Whit Sunday (First Sunday in June)
- National Day (June 6)
- Midsummer's Day (Changeable: Saturday late June)
- All Saints' Day (Saturday between Oct 31 and Nov 6)
- Christmas Eve (Dec 24)
- Christmas Day (Dec 25)
- 2nd Day of Christmas (Dec 26)

---

2   Information via http://publicholidays.eu/sweden/

Natural Disasters

There have not been any serious natural disasters in Sweden causing lasting damage. Hurricanes, flooding, landslides, and avalanches have all occurred in the past, but Sweden has a good safety record and strong policy for reducing natural hazards and disaster risks across the country. County Administrative Boards and municipalities have adaptation measures in place and work to prevent and reduce the consequences of natural disasters, supported by the MBA (Swedish Civil Contingencies Agency). Therefore, it is highly unlikely that your time on the Kungsleden will be affected by such.

Fjällräven Classic

This is a huge hiking event that takes place in August ever year, where around 2,000 people from over 30 countries descend on the northern part of the Kungsleden, hiking 110 kilometres (68 miles) from the Sámi village of Nikkaluokta through to Abisko, making it the busiest section of the trail during the summer season.

STF Accommodation – Seasonal Opening Hours

Along the Kungsleden, the winter season runs from the end of February to the end of April or beginning of May. The summer season runs from Midsummer's Day until the middle or end of September. During both seasons, the opening hours of the Fjällstations and mountain huts may differ from one region to the next, so it is advisable to check your preferred dates on the STF website during the initial planning stages of your trip.

Link: *https://www.swedishtouristassociation.com/staying-at-an-stf-mountain-cabin/*

The STF mountain huts are typically closed between seasons, but safety facilities are available at all times. It is therefore still possible to spend the night in a hut, but the gas supply will be closed and access to the kitchen and firewood will be limited. If an emergency telephone is available, it can be used to contact the mountain rescue services if necessary.

3. Long Lead Items

Arranging a multi-day backpacking trip on the Kungsleden involves several steps, some requiring more lead time than others. This chapter introduces the most important items that require advance thinking and preparation in order to have a more successful and enjoyable journey. Considering factors such as transport and accommodation early on in the planning process, for example, may mean you can take advantage of 'early bird deals' with advance bookings, so you can make great savings.

a. Permits & Regulations

Obtaining a permit is traditionally one of the first long lead items to consider when planning a thru-hike. However, you do not need a permit to complete the Kungsleden or sections of the trail. This factor instantly saves you time and money, as there is no application process needed for access to the trail and, similarly, no fee required to enter a Swedish national park. Allemansrätten, or "Everyone's Right", therefore, is yet another element that makes Sweden such an attractive destination for the outdoor enthusiast.

Providing a unique freedom of access to Sweden's countryside and wilderness areas, Allemansrätten has become an integral part of the Swedish national identity. The origins of the *Right* date back to the local laws and customs of the Middle Ages, and it is of enormous importance to both individuals and groups. School groups, for example, explore the forests from an early age, and families often fish, pick berries, or go for walks in the woods together. However, with these rights come certain responsibilities following the principles of "do not disturb, do not destroy".

Despite the freedoms and rights that Allemansrätten affords, in protected areas, such as national parks and nature reserves, there are special rules and regulations designed to protect valuable natural and cultural features. Sweden has 29 national parks covering a total area of 731,589 hectares, five of which you will pass through along the 430-kilometre (267 miles) Kungsleden route. From north to south these are: Abisko, Pieljekaise, Stora Sjöfallet, Padjelanta, and Sarek, the latter three forming part of the UNESCO World Heritage Site of Laponia. Established in 1909, Sarek was Sweden's first national park and the first of its kind in Europe.

Some rules restrict the Right of Public Access, while others expand it. The regulations, which must be observed by everybody, including the landowner, vary from one area to another depending on what is necessary to preserve the features of the particular area. When hiking through areas with specific regulations, you must see notices for information. The regulations governing nature reserves and national parks are often printed in English on a noticeboard near the entrance. They can also be found in English on the website of the Swedish EPA (Environment Protection Agency).

Link: *http://www.swedishepa.se/Enjoying-nature/Protected-areas/ National-Parks/*

The regulations applying to nature reserves can be obtained from the local municipality or county administrative board that established the reserve. The county administrative board can also provide other information, such as which times of year you may not enter the county's bird and seal sanctuaries.

b. Hiking Buddy

You may feel completely comfortable with hiking solo and enjoy the sheer amount of freedom that comes with it. You get to hike on your own schedule without having to compromise, negotiate, or consider the needs of anyone else. Yet, having a hiking companion could be very beneficial to the successful completion of your thru-hike for a number of reasons as well.

If you are on a tight budget, hiking with a partner or buddy could enable you to split certain costs, e.g., for transport and accommodation. Sharing essential items of equipment can further reduce your initial costs of gear that is not previously owned and additionally help minimise individual pack weight.

Another clear benefit is that teamwork makes a whole lot of trail tasks much easier – from putting up a tent, fetching and filtering water, taking turns to cook, to simply having someone to take your photo in that idyllic location. It also makes your journey a shared experience that you can discuss and muse over for many years to come.

When hiking with a companion or as part of a group over a long period of time, you will inevitably develop a real sense of camaraderie. One that you may never have experienced at any other time in your life. Out there on the trail, you will hopefully be with like-minded people that share your sense of adventure and love for the great outdoors. Swapping hiking tales around the camp stove or sharing tips and inspiring others to visit places they have not yet been to over a pint or two is likely to be the order of the day.

On a long-distance hike of this magnitude, it is also very reassuring to know that you are hiking with another, particularly when hiking through the more remote regions, where interactions with other walkers or communities may be minimal. Knowing there is someone else to confer with when the trail is not obvious or when you arrive at a poorly marked junction provides you with an added sense of security.

Of course, there are also disadvantages to hiking with someone else or being part of a large group of hikers on the trail. In order to have a pleasant experience, you've all got to get along, muck in, be fair, and accept a group majority, even if it's not really your thing.

If you are considering hiking with a guided group or joining a group tour, bear in mind the itinerary is usually set. You don't have the flexibility as with planning your own trip. There's no option to stay at a campsite for an extra night to take a side trip or simply deciding you will set off an hour later to stay in bed longer, especially if you have cooking duties to take care of. Group responsibilities come before your own needs. If you are someone who likes flexibility, then hiking with a guided group is probably not for you.

Similarly, if solitude is important to you, then constant company may dampen the experience and put a strain on your relationship. You will need to find some balance between hiking well together and enjoying the mutual company, while still having your own space so as not to become tired of or stressed by each other. Different hiking paces can also affect the partnership. It can be frustrating to slow down to accommodate someone else's more moderate pace. Likewise, pushing harder to achieve someone else's faster pace can cause injury.

The most important thing is to know the kind of person you are on the trail and to pinpoint your strengths and weaknesses. If you prefer to do things your own way, you may find hiking with a companion or as part of a group both frustrating and overbearing. If you like the reassurance of having someone else with you while hiking, carefully consider all options before deciding who that someone else is going to be. You'll be in close proximity with this person for several days, so it is imperative that you get along.

As a married couple who love to hike, we both have clearly defined roles when it comes to navigation, camp setup, and certain routines. We get along for the most part, but even with lots of experience and good organisation, we can still have our moments when we're suffering from hunger and fatigue. Taking all of the above into consideration, our top piece of advice is to choose your hiking buddy wisely!

c. Travel Arrangements

Getting to the start of the trail and back from the end point takes some planning. Depending on where you are coming from and in which direction you plan to walk the route, there are different options to consider. Lapland is relatively remote but surprisingly easy to reach from cosmopolitan Stockholm. Additionally, Kiruna makes a laid-back staging city, accessed by air, with convenient bus connections to and from different trail access points. An overview of major towns and train routes across the country as well as airport connections is provided below.

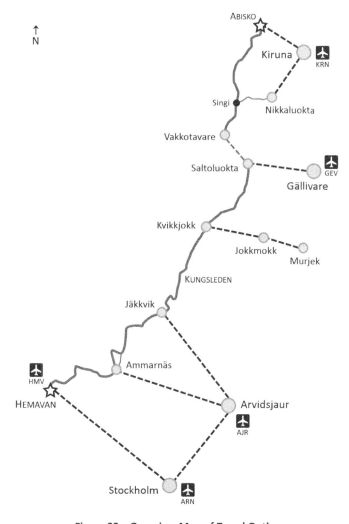

Figure 22 – Overview Map of Travel Options

Starting in Hemavan (South)

If you plan to hike the Kungsleden in the alternate direction going south to north, such as we did, your journey will start from the small ski town of Hemavan and Tärnaby.

By Air: If you are travelling from outside of Sweden, it is likely that you'll land in Stockholm. There are direct daily flights to Stockholm Arlanda Airport (ARN) from principal airports around the world throughout the summer season. The quickest way to get from Stockholm to Hemavan and Tärnaby (HMV) is to take a domestic flight, journey time approximately 3 hours. (Tickets can be purchased in advance online from low-cost Swedish airline NextJet, *http://www.nextjet.se/en.*)

By Rail: Taking the train entails buying a special ticket (*Resplusbiljett*) which combines train and long-distance bus travel. If you are coming from southern Sweden, choose between trains heading for Östersund, Vännäs, or Umeå, and then a connecting bus service will take you on to Tärnaby, then Hemavan. You can make reservations by contacting: *www.sj.se* (+46 (0) 771 75 75 75)

By Road: Long-distance bus services *(Länstrafikens Bussar)* exist across the country, and it is possible to find connections to almost all towns in Sweden. For example, travelling between Hemavan and Tärnaby and Umeå, there are several departures daily. The trip takes about five hours. You can make reservations by contacting: *www.tabussen.nu* (+ 46 (0) 771 100 110)

Lapplandspilen is a direct coach service to and from Stockholm that departs from the centre of the city several times a week. The night coach takes just under 14 hours. You can make reservations by contacting: *www. lapplandspilen.se* (+46 (0) 940 150 30)

Note: Some buses only run during the summer season. Hemavan is also easily accessible by car from Umeå or Mo i Rana in Norway.

Starting in Abisko (North)

Alternatively, if you intend to hike the Kungsleden southbound in the traditional direction, you will start from the northernmost point at Abisko.

By Air: Abisko does not have its own airport, therefore, if you are travelling from outside Sweden, it is likely you will connect via Stockholm (Arlanda airport, ARN) or Kiruna (Kiruna airport, KRN). SAS and Norwegian Air operate flights to Kiruna. As Abisko lies approximately 100 kilometres west of Kiruna, it may be more convenient to fly to Kiruna instead of the capital city for quicker connections by road or rail.

By Rail: Access to Abisko is by direct train from Gothenburg, Stockholm, or Narvik. Two overnight trains run from central Stockholm through to Abisko, journey time 18 hours and 40 minutes. Trains stop at Arlanda airport for passengers to board. Prices vary depending on standard class, comfort, or sleeper. Alternatively, from Kiruna to Abisko, the train journey takes a little over an hour. However, there are only a couple of services per day. Tickets are usually available 90 days before departure, so book ahead to get the best prices. (+46 (0) 771 75 75 75; *www.sj.se*)

By Road: Long-distance and regional bus services operate between Stockholm and Kiruna (21 hours) and Kiruna and Abisko. You can make reservations by contacting Länstrafikens Bussar (+46 (0) 771 100 110; *www.ltnbd.se*) or Kiruna Buss (+46 (0) 980-12 400; *info@kirunabuss.se*). The bus trip from the Kiruna bus station to the Abisko tourist station takes about 1 hour and 15 minutes.

From the UK, we flew direct to Stockholm, then on to Hemavan in one day, and started the trail the following morning. After completing the Kungsleden, we stayed for one night in Abisko Östra, then took the overnight train (boarding at Abisko Östra station) back to Stockholm, disembarking at Arlanda airport to return to the UK. (Note that the airport enforces a mandatory station passage fee of an additional 85 SEK (£7) if your train ticket is for Stockholm Central.)

Due to timings and connections depending on where you are travelling from, ideally allow for a travel day at either end of your trip. The cost of tickets by both air and by rail depend on many factors. Generally, booking as early as possible to secure your preferred date will also mean you will get tickets at the best price.

[i] The STF provides basic information in English and Japanese and much more in Swedish and European languages. STF volunteers answer email. If you enquire in English about a travel detail or ask a question about the Kungsleden, you usually get a response in English within a week or so.

Local Connections/Trailhead Options

If you intend on hiking just a section of the Kungsleden, there are a few places along the trail that can be reached by road or public transport. Additionally, a few others can also be reached by boat charter services.

Below is a list of the most common choices:

If you want to start from Saltoluokta, Suorva and Kebnats can be reached by bus or car from Gällivare (1 hour 20 minutes). A train journey from Kiruna to Gällivare (1 hour 10 minutes), then continuing by bus (Line 93) and boat to Saltoluokta is the most common mode here. Domestic flights are also available from Stockholm to Gällivare.

If you opt to take a detour off the Kungsleden to Kebnekaise, Nikkaluokta can be reached by bus or car from Kiruna. Kvikkjokk can be reached by bus (Line 94) or car from Jokkmokk. Jäkkvik can be reached by bus or car from Umeå, Arvidsjaur, or Fauske in Norway. Adolfström can be reached by bus or car from Arjeplog. Ammarnäs can be reached by bus or car from Sorsele. Kvikkjokk to Ammarnäs: Bus from Murjek/Jokkmokk to Kvikkjokk. Bus from Vännäs to Ammarnäs.

From	To	Type	Cost (SEK)
Stockholm	Hemavan	Flight	1,750-2,000
Stockholm	Arvidsjaur	Flight	750-1,800
Stockholm	Gällivare	Flight	800-1,900
Stockholm	Kiruna	Flight	600-2,300
Stockholm	Abisko	Night Train	1,000-2,400
Arvidsjaur	Sorsele	Bus 25	80-140
Sorsele	Ammarnäs	Bus 341	60-95
Arvidsjaur	Arjeplog	Bus 17	110-140
Arjeplog	Jäkkvik	Bus 104	95-120
Murjek	Kvikkjokk	Bus 94	300-400
Murjek	Gällivare	Train	100-210
Gällivare	Saltoluokta	Bus 93	200-300
Gällivare	Vakkotavare	Bus 93	200-300
Kiruna	Nikkaluokta	Bus 92	120-160
Kiruna	Abisko	Train	70-110
Kiruna	Abisko	Bus 91	120-170

Table 4 – Transportation Options between Entry/Exit Points

d. Trail Shelters

At the start and end of your thru-hike and in the few towns and villages along the route, there are more lodging options to consider than when you're out on the trail in the backcountry. This includes the provision of campsites with full amenities and having a few more home comforts by way of staying in a hostel or hotel. Otherwise, you will find that accommodation along the Kungsleden is generally simple in nature.

STF Mountain Huts

If camping isn't your first choice, the Swedish Tourist Association (STF) operates a series of huts and cabins across the mountainous regions of Sweden that serve your basic needs. On most of the Kungsleden route, you will find that these huts are conveniently located within a day's walk of each other.

Typically, each hut complex consists of a series of buildings spread across a small area. Inside the huts, there is a large kitchen/dining area and separate dorm-style rooms for sleeping, usually with 4-6 beds (triple bunks) in each. A pillow and blanket are provided, so if you're not camping, you only have to carry a light sleep sheet. Some bedrooms also have wood burning stoves for warmth. Furnishings in the common area include wooden tables and chairs, candles, and there are usually a few pictures on the walls of Swedish flora and fauna. There may also be a shelf with books and games for your entertainment. Often, there are separate huts for people hiking with dogs and these are also available for day use where hikers can use the facilities for a fee between the hours of 11:00 AM and 3:00 PM. (Day use is free if you have an STF membership card.) Long-drop toilets are located outside with supplies of toilet paper, hand cleaning gel, and soap.

Figure 23 – Typical STF Mountain Hut | Toilet Block with Wash Basin & Hand Sanitiser

The huts have no electricity, running water, or any other modern amenities, but, despite this fact, every hut is well-equipped and follows the same procedures. Everyone who stays in the huts or uses their facilities is responsible for their upkeep. In the kitchen area, there are large buckets that are denoted as 'blue' or 'red' for collecting fresh water from a nearby river/spring, denoted by a sign *'vatten'*, and disposing of waste water by emptying it into a special drainage container outside, referred to as the *'slask'*, usually located near the pit toilets. It is your responsibility to refill/ empty water if you have used it. You are also expected to chop wood in the wood shed to maintain a good supply for the kitchen stove (and sauna if the hut has one).

A substantial wood burning stove warms the dining area and large pans of water that are placed on top. This hot water is then used for washing up. A large kitchen unit houses pots and pans, crockery and utensils, and gas stoves for cooking are positioned on each work top. All items can be used as long as they are washed and returned. Similarly, counters should be wiped and stoves cleaned. Beds need to be made and floors swept. All rubbish should be sorted in various bins according to type, with anything non-recyclable burnt on site, and the rest hauled away during winter.

Figure 24 – Typical Kitchen Setup | Dining Area & Day Use Facilities

During the hiking season, each hut is staffed with a warden, and most huts have facilities, such as a small shop (*butik*) for supplies, a drying room (*tork*), and sometimes a sauna (*bastu*). (Bear in mind, each shop varies in amount and variety of supplies, and selection gets thin as the season nears the end.) One of the key features we tended to use a lot was the drying room. In every mountain hut, these rooms are equipped with a burner to keep the space heated and have several wash lines and wooden racks on either side to hang your gear, so that you can quickly and efficiently dry it out. We found these invaluable along the route as we frequently had wet gear. After a cold, rainy day of hiking, the warmth of a fire and the ability to dry your clothes is a welcome reward!

Another feature of the huts we started to use regularly was the sauna. The saunas follow a procedure whereby there are typically three sessions per evening: women, men, and mixed sessions at specific times. Starting around 5:00-6:00 PM in the evening is the norm. A relaxing sit and chat in a sauna, perhaps combined with a brisk dip into a nearby river or lake, is often a rewarding finish to a day of hiking. Even if you don't intend on using the sauna, there is a plentiful supply of hot water, perfect for washing yourself after a day on the trail.

[!] It is important to keep the opening dates for the mountain huts in mind, as almost all additional public transport revolves around this seasonal period. If you are section-hiking and arrive in Nikkaluokta a few days too late, you may find that there's no longer a bus running to take you back to Kiruna!

The huts on the northern loop of the trail remain open approximately one week longer than in the south. Exact opening times can be found on the STF website.

Link: *https://www.swedishtouristassociation.com/staying-at-an-stf-mountain-cabin/*

STF Fjällstation

An STF Fjällstation (mountain station/lodge) is different to a mountain hut. Only located near entry points of the trail and often in the vicinity of nature reserves and national parks, these are fully-serviced lodges complete with electricity, running water, showers, restaurant, shop, Wi-Fi, and more, thereby providing a mixture of comforts associated with a hotel, hostel, or guest house. Along the Kungsleden, Fjällstations can be found at Hemavan, Kvikkjokk, Saltoluokta, Kebnekaise, and Abisko.

Figure 25 – Fjällstation Reception Area| Lounge Area with Wi-Fi

STF Membership

You do not need to be an STF member to stay in the huts or Fjällstationer. However, if you are planning to utilise the huts each night, then we recommend joining the STF. A membership will save you 100 SEK per night, which can be a considerable amount over three or four weeks.

The following prices quoted are for the time of our hike in 2016, with approximate conversions to GBP. As exchange rates fluctuate and prices may increase year on year, check current prices on the STF website before you travel. Currently, membership with the STF costs 295 SEK (£25) per year for adults aged 26 years or over. Youth members of 16-25 years have a discounted rate of 150 SEK (£13). You can sign up online (make sure it is long enough in advance of your trip to receive your membership card) or you can become a member at any of the mountain stations along the trail (Hemavan, Kvikkjokk, Saltoluokta, Kebnekaise, Abisko), at which point you will receive a temporary card for your hike. Note that residents outside of Sweden will be charged an additional postage fee of 140 SEK (£12) for members in Europe, or 185 SEK (£16) for members outside of Europe to cover postage of the STF tourist magazine.

The nightly fee differs between STF accommodations, depending on what part of the trail you are traveling on. For the summer season, all mountain huts except for the northern part of the Kungsleden charge 460 SEK (£40) for non-members and 360 SEK (£31) for members of the STF. To stay at STF huts in the north (Singi, Sälka, Tjäktja, Alesjaure, and Abiskojaure), you will pay an additional 50 SEK (£4.50), as these are the more popular huts. (Members: 410 SEK (£35.50)/Non-members: 510 SEK (£44).) Expect to pay considerably more to stay at a Fjällstation, where prices are typically doubled as you have access to more facilities.

Accepted Payment Methods

While many of the huts along the route can now accept credit card payments, not all can. Therefore, it is better to carry enough cash to cover your accommodation. (It is possible to purchase credit vouchers at the Fjällstationer along the trail if you find your cash reserves are running low.) Unlike at the Fjällstationer, it is not possible to make reservations prior to arrival at STF mountain huts. They operate on a first-come, first-served basis. However, if a hut happens to be full, wardens ensure that you will get a mattress with some space somewhere on the floor to sleep.

It is possible to camp in the nearby vicinity of the mountain huts and pay a reduced fee. This is 100 SEK (£9) per person/night for members and 200 SEK (£18) for non-members. This allows you use of one of the buildings, typically designated for campers, with common area and kitchen. You also have access to the sauna, should there be one. This is a popular option that many people use to save money, while still maintaining most of the convenience of the huts. Similarly, it is possible to pay a day use fee at Fjällstations to take advantage of the extra facilities available, which is a good option if you don't want to pay for overnight accommodation. For example, at Kvikkjokk Fjällstation, day use is 150 SEK (£13) per person. If you only want to take a shower or use the hostel kitchen, there are also separate fees. (Showers are 40 SEK/£3.50, hostel kitchen is 40 SEK/£3.50.)

[i] If you are already a member of *Hostelling International* and can produce your membership card, you will receive the same benefits and discounts as an STF member! If you reside in the UK, join the YHA for a year's family membership for £25, which automatically includes the Hostelling International membership. This is far cheaper than purchasing the STF card online or when you arrive at a Fjällstation.

Emergency Shelters

In addition to the STF mountain huts, there are several basic emergency shelters spread across the trail, typically at mountain passes. These are not meant to be used as accommodation when you don't feel like camping. They're only to be used in an actual emergency situation. They are, however, useful places to stop for a rest and eat lunch out of the wind and rain. Often at emergency shelters, you will also find an emergency telephone (usually marked on your map) with direct contact to the local police, should it be necessary.

Figure 26 – Modern Emergency Shelter Interior | Traditional Lappish Shelter

A full list of accommodation options available along the Kungsleden route is given in the table below (south-to-north direction).

Location	Accommodation Type	Cumulative Distance (km/mi)	Camping (fee)	Shop	Sauna	Laundry	Card Payment	Wi-Fi	Recharge Point
Hemavan	Fjällstation	0	√	√	√	√	√	√	√
Viterskalet	Mtn. Hut	11/7	√	√			√		
Syter	Mtn. Hut	23/14	√	√			√		
Tärnasjö	Mtn. Hut	37/23	√	√	√				
Serve	Mtn. Hut	51/32	√	√					
Aigert	Mtn. Hut	70/44	√	√	√				
Ammarnäs	Mtn. Hut	78/49	√	√	√	√	√	√	√
Rävfallsstugan	Mtn. Hut	97/61	√		√				
Sjnulttjie	Mountain Shelter	124/78	√						
Bäverholmen	Hostel	138/86	√	√			√		√
Adolfström	Holiday Village	145/91	√	√	√	√	√		√
Jäkkvik	Hostel	166/104	√	√	√	√	√	√	√
Vuonatjviken	Holiday Village	184/115					√		√
Kvikkjokk	Fjällstation	249/156	√	√	√	√	√	√	√
Pårte	Mtn. Hut	265/166	√						
Aktse	Mtn. Hut	289/181	√	√			√		
Sitojaure	Mtn. Hut	302/189	√						
Saltoluokta	Fjällstation	322/201	√	√	√		√	√	√
Vakkotavare*	Mtn. Hut	0/0	√	√			√		
Teusajaure	Mtn. Hut	338/211	√		√		√		
Kaitumjaure	Mtn. Hut	347/217	√	√	√		√		
Singi	Mtn. Hut	360/225	√						
Sälka	Mtn. Hut	372/233	√	√	√				
Tjäktja	Mtn. Hut	384/240	√						
Alesjaure	Mtn. Hut	397/247	√	√	√		√		
Abiskojaure	Mtn. Hut	417/260	√	√	√		√		
Abisko	Fjällstation	432/269	√	√	√	√	√	√	√

* Saltoluokta to Vakkotavare is via the boat/bus service (-> zero hiking kilometres).

Table 5 – Trail Shelter Options in South-to-North Direction

Note: Rävfallsstugan is a locked cabin provided by the County Administrative Board of Västerbotten. If you intend on using it as overnight accommodation to break up this section, you will need to book a bed, pay the fee, and collect a key from the Vindelfjällen Naturum Centre or the Ammarnäsgården Fjällhotell when passing through Ammarnäs. The key can then be deposited in Adolfström. Further details are given in the *Contact Information* section of the appendix.

Figure 27 – Kungsleden Trail Shelters

4. Planning & Preparation

So you've decided to go for it and walk the Kungsleden in its entirety! 430 kilometres is no easy task, but with great challenge comes great reward. To help you achieve your goal, proper planning and preparation will be key to successfully completing and fully enjoying this thru-hike. You can do this in manageable stages, using the guidance provided in this chapter, and subsequently plunge into this great outdoor adventure with the confidence that everything is properly taken care of.

a. Itinerary

In general, the itinerary planning process can be broken down into two stages. The first stage includes all activities concerning long lead items, such as travel arrangements and accommodation. The resulting 'macro-plan' is the logistical frame of your trip. The second stage focuses on determining the specifics of your thru-hike, such as daily distances, desired campsites, and resupply. The resulting 'micro-plan' is your personal hiking itinerary.

Macro-Planning

The below flow chart outlines the important steps in planning the logistics of your trip. The order shown was determined based on pragmatic considerations and may be altered depending on personal preferences. Individual steps may also be omitted if not applicable.

Figure 28 – Flow Chart Macro-Planning

First, you should estimate your trail days. Be realistic about what you can achieve in terms of daily mileage and ensure that the schedule you set for yourself is right for you. The resulting duration of your hike will impact all of the subsequent macro-planning decisions. Once you know how long it will take you to hike the Kungsleden, check your calendar for times that you would be able to go. Cross-reference your schedule with those of any hiking buddies and make a list of all the date ranges that will work for your group. Once you have selected and confirmed a date, it is time to get started on travel arrangements, especially when you are planning to arrive from an international location.

The next step is to decide on your preferred type of accommodation – camping, lodging, or a combination of both. This decision will likely be influenced by seasonal aspects, such as weather, public holidays, and your overall budget. Whilst it is not possible to book beds in the STF mountain huts along the trail (first-come, first-served only), you can make reservations at the Fjällstations.

To coincide with travel arrangements, you may wish to stay in a Fjällstation at the beginning and end of your hike. Similarly, if you plan on using a Fjällstation to take any rest days or side trips, it is advisable to book ahead as they get very busy with tour groups, vacationers, and other people walking the Kungsleden. This does mean you will have to stick to your itinerary, leaving less room for flexibility, as you will have to reach certain distances within a given time.

Upon completion of the macro-planning step, you will have the following:

- Rough hiking schedule (starting and ending date)
- Transportation plan to the trailhead at Hemavan (or Abisko)
- Transportation plan from the trailhead at Abisko (or Hemavan)
- Accommodations before and after your hike (if required)
- Accommodations along the route (if required)

Micro-Planning

With your starting and ending dates decided, the goal of this planning stage is to map out your personal hiking strategy by breaking down your time on the trail into segments that will dictate your campsite locations and daily mileage. General considerations are your personal hiking speed, availability of water, the amount of food you intend to carry, when and where you plan to resupply, difficulty of the terrain, and your preferred accommodation options.

Along the Kungsleden, even in the remoter, less frequented sections, you should never have any real difficulty with topping up your drinking water supplies or resupplying food, as you will pass numerous watercourses and predominantly arrive at an STF mountain hut each day. Even if you do not intend to camp at the hut or use it for overnight accommodation, you are able to access fresh water and use the toilets. Most huts also have a shop where you can stock up with basic food rations, so you will only need to carry food for a few days at a time.

Whilst there are few significant elevation gains or losses on the Kungsleden, the first step is to determine how far you will be able to travel each day and pick out preferred campsite locations, whether it be at an STF hut or wild camping. As the distance between mountain huts is usually a comfortable day walk of between 12 and 15 kilometres (7-9 miles), you can use the huts as reference points and pick out potential campsites close to their location, also considering the terrain if you prefer to wild camp. Both the overview of STF accommodation with established campsites and the elevation profiles of the trail provided in Appendix A are great tools to aid you in this effort.

[i] Remember that there are no STF huts between Ammarnäs and Kvikkjokk, which is a section of the Kungsleden of approximately 130 kilometres (81 miles). If you are intending on completing the entire route, there is private accommodation available in Bäverholmen, Adolfström, Jäkkvik, and Vuonatjviken. Apart from some basic unmanned shelters for use in emergency, your only other option is to wild camp.

Essentially, planning your detailed itinerary comes down to individual hiking speed and preferred accommodation option. You can either estimate the distance based on your experience from previous hiking trips or calculate your average daily mileage as outlined in Section 1b *Time*, incorporating the difficulty of a particular trail section as per elevation profile.

To support you with this, there are three suggested itineraries for the Kungsleden given below based on a fast (21 days), moderate (26 days), and relaxed pace (32 days).

Location	Fast		Moderate		Relaxed	
	day	km (miles)	day	km (miles)	day	km (miles)
Hemavan	-	-	-	-	-	-
Viterskalet			1	11 (6.8)	1	11 (6.8)
Syter	1	23 (14.3)	2	12 (7.5)	2	12 (7.5)
Tärnasjö			3	14 (8.7)	3	14 (8.7)
Serve	2	28 (17.4)	4	14 (8.7)	4	14 (8.7)
Vuomatjåhkka						
Juovvatjåhkka					6	11 (6.8)
Aigert	3	19 (11.8)	5	19 (11.8)	6	8 (5)
Ammarnäs	4	8 (5)	6	8 (5)	7	8 (5)
Rävfallsstugan	5	19 (11.8)	7	19 (11.8)	8	19 (11.8)
Lisvuojávrrie*					9	10 (6.2)

Sjnulttjie	6	27 (16.8)	8	27 (16.8)	10	17 (10.5)
Badasjåkkå			9	11 (6.8)		
Bäverholmen					11	14 (8.7)
Adolfström	7	21 (13)	10	10 (6.2)	12	7 (4.3)
Pieljekaisestugan						
Jäkkvik	8	21 (13)	11	21 (13)	13	21 (13)
Vuonatjviken	9	18 (11.2)	12	18 (11.2)	14	18 (11.2)
Tjaurkatan*	10	21 (13)	13	21 (13)	15	21 (13)
Goabddabakte*	11	22 (13.7)	14	22 (13.7)	16	22 (13.7)
Tsielekjakkstugan						
Kvikkjokk	12	22 (13.7)	15	22 (13.7)	17	22 (13.7)
Pårte	13	16 (9.9)	16	16 (9.9)	18	16 (9.9)
Jagge					19	9 (5.6)
Aktse	14	25 (15.5)	17	25 (15.5)	20	16 (9.9)
Sitojaure	15	13 (8.1)	18	13 (8.1)	21	13 (8.1)
Áutsutjvágge					22	11 (6.8)
Saltoluokta	16	20 (12.4)	19	20 (12.4)	23	9 (5.6)
Vakkotavare**			20	0 (0)	24	0 (0)
Teusajaure	17	16 (9.9)	21	16 (9.9)	25	16 (9.9)
Kaitumjaure			22	9 (5.6)	26	9 (5.6)
Singi	18	22 (13.7)			27	13 (8.1)
Sälka			23	25 (15.5)	28	12 (7.5)
Tjäktja	19	24 (14.9)			29	12 (7.5)
Alesjaure			24	25 (15.5)	30	13 (8.1)
Rádunjárga	20	20 (12.4)				
Abiskojaure			25	20 (12.4)	31	20 (12.4)
Abisko	21	28 (17.4)	26	15 (9.3)	32	15 (9.3)

* Wild camping locations; no huts or cabins.
** Saltoluokta to Vakkotavare is via the boat/bus service (-> zero hiking kilometres).

Table 6 – Sample Itineraries based on Fast, Moderate, and Relaxed Pace

[i] It is advisable to create a slower "Plan B" schedule of alternate trip legs and campsites so that you can adjust your schedule while on the trail if you find your original schedule was too aggressive or optimistic.

b. Food

Food should not be underestimated in its ability to revive energy and keep spirits up. Looking forward to a good meal on the trail is motivational and having a satisfied stomach lets you fall asleep more contentedly at night. Putting effort into planning and preparing balanced meals with a lot of variety is well worth it. There's nothing worse than eating a meal that brings you little enjoyment. Refer to Appendix F for a comprehensive list of food suggestions.

Below are some guidelines for choosing the right kind of food when planning your trail menu:

- Nutritional value: choose high energy foods and ensure an adequate supply of vitamins and minerals

- Calorie distribution: balance approximately 15% protein, 60% carbohydrates, and 25% fat per meal

- Non-perishable: your food must not spoil for a week or longer at up to 30°C (90°F)

- Weight: your food should be as dry and light as possible (including packaging)

- Ease of preparation: save gas, time, dirty pots, and nerves after a long day of hiking

Two factors are particularly important to consider when determining how much food to bring on your journey: calorie value and pack space. Your meals should provide approximately 1.5-2 times the calories you usually consume per day. Calculate higher calories when in low temperatures, and vice versa. Additional hunger can be satisfied with snacks. As on any multi-day backpacking trip, pack space is always at a premium. Make sure all food items have a dense nutritional value and are worth their weight and space. The less space you have, the less water and air content should be in your food packaging.

[i] As a rule of thumb, try to aim for 3,000-3,500 calories per person/day. For a more personalized figure, look up the *Harris-Benedict Equation*.

In order to avoid space issues, it helps to repackage your food into single servings, let out any air, and cut off excess packaging. Zip lock bags work well, as they can be labelled and reused for packing out waste. As you pack your food into a dry bag, try to make layers of meals per day rather than packing all breakfasts at the bottom, and so forth. This makes accessing your food more convenient. Furthermore, pack the most perishable food items at the top of your bag for early consumption.

In addition to your main meals, well-chosen snacks and supplements can provide valuable nourishment. As temperatures rise, it is vital to replenish electrolytes, such as sodium, chloride, potassium, magnesium, manganese, and calcium, on a consistent basis. High water intake without electrolyte replacement over many hours can lead to *hyponatremia*, a life-threatening condition where your body does not have enough salts to function. Adding salty snacks (crisps, salted nuts, savoury crackers, or pretzels) and/or supplements to your trail diet helps avoid electrolyte imbalance.

[!] If you are on a low sodium diet, ask your doctor if a higher sodium intake while on the trail would be appropriate for you.

As you plan your meals, mind the respective cooking times and utensils needed for preparation. Anything that requires boiling for over ten minutes can be bothersome and can consume too much fuel. Similarly, excessive in-camp preparations, such as cutting, peeling, and mashing, or meals that require a lot of attention can be a hassle when you're exhausted or overly hungry. Many hikers plan their meals so that the only cooking gear required is a small gas stove, one pot, and one spoon. Nevertheless, whatever meals you decide to go with, bring along adequate equipment and know your tolerance for cooking and cleaning dishes in the backcountry. Of the many things to enjoy on this experience, consider whether you want cooking to be one of them. Will it be relaxing or feel like a chore? Plan your meals accordingly.

[i] A good tip for the morning is to eat a quick cereal bar for breakfast, warm up while packing up, and get going faster to save time and gas needed for a hot breakfast later.

You may decide to alternate your food strategy depending on the difficulty of the day ahead, the campsite you are staying at, the arrival time, or whether you intend on using the facilities provided by the STF huts. For example, all huts have kitchen facilities whereby you can use gas for cooking. You might even take advantage of a ready-made evening meal or buffet breakfast by dining in the restaurant if you pass a Fjällstation. Similarly, scenic spots and shorter trail days may invite you to enjoy a relaxing morning coffee or spend a long evening with celebratory dining around the campfire. In summary, your food strategy is a matter of your personal preference, the tightness of your schedule, access to food and gas, and your resupply strategy.

c. Resupply

Unlike other long-distance wilderness hikes where access to food on the trail may be limited as you spend several days away from civilisation, the Swedish Tourist Association have made it possible to purchase food at regular intervals along the Kungsleden by providing small resupply shops in most of the mountain huts. This allows you more flexibility with meal options and means, for the most part, you will only have to carry a couple of day's food rations at a time. The shops are known as *butik* and are often located at the warden's office. Each shop varies in the amount and variety of supplies, but generally you will find that the bigger, more popular huts have a better selection of goods. Bear in mind that this selection gets more limited as the season nears the end.

Along the route, settlements tend to have at least one shop – whether it be a small grocery store or larger supermarket – and all have a general selection of easy-to-cook foods, catering to passing hikers. Hemavan and Abisko have the largest supermarkets, generally open 10:00 AM to 8:00 PM except Sundays, and stock a wider variety of goods. So you may want to plan meal options ahead of time and stock up on essentials that will be more difficult to get a hold of further along the trail.

Other good resupply options are Ammarnäs and Jäkkvik. As well as stocking a good variety of foods for hiking, both have other essentials, such as replacement gear (e.g., gas, socks, and sunglasses) and medical supplies. Bäverholmen has a restaurant/café that sells some supplies and snacks, and Adolfström also has several restaurants and a small shop. This shop has limited opening hours, especially during the latter part of the season, so don't rely on being able to resupply there.

Figure 29 – Typical Food Supplies in Small STF Huts | Kaitumjaure STF Hut Shop

Generally in the STF huts, food is limited to tinned and packet goods, which are transported by snowmobile or helicopter during the winter months. Therefore, expect to pay inflated prices, sometimes three times as much as that of the supermarket. In the south, the shop inside the warden's hut at Viter, although small, has a good food selection, and you can pay by card. In the north, the STF huts Kaitumjaure and Alesjaure have larger shops with more provisions, and it is also possible to pay by card. Kvikkjokk and Saltoluokta Fjällstations have large, well-stocked grocery stores with similar selections, but goods carry inflated prices as with the mountain huts. Note, the further north you go, the less option there is to purchase fresh food stuffs, unless you shop or dine at a Fjällstation.

Food stuffs that you can purchase along the trail typically include tinned fish, meatballs, goulash, beans, and soups, packets of instant noodles, pasta, pasta sauces, rice and potatoes, cereals, nuts and dried fruit, chocolate bars, jelly sweets, biscuits, crackers, and crisps. We took our own milk powder, although it is possible to buy this along the trail in some STF shops, too. In the huts, tinned foods are relatively expensive, for example, large tins of meatballs or goulash are around 60 SEK (£5), whereas packets of instant noodles are approximately 20 SEK (£1.75). Additionally, huts sell cans of fizzy drinks and beer.

Your budget will influence whether you can splash out on a tin of Swedish meatballs or have to stick to instant noodles. So for variety, you may decide that it is worth buying some supplies from a supermarket at the start of your hike to post on to a Fjällstation or hut served by a road further along the trail. The postal service in Sweden is relatively inexpensive, so you may still save money compared with buying food in the huts. For example, we used the post office in Hemavan to forward on our hand luggage to Abisko, cared for by the hostel we would be staying at on completion of the trail. The cost to post the case with contents of around 4 kilograms (9 pounds) was 167 SEK (£15). You can make this decision when you arrive in Sweden and check out current prices to choose the best option for you.

More information can be found on the STF website if you check under specific accommodation. For example, the Kvikkjokk Fjällstation accepts parcels marked with your name and the date when you expect to collect it. Depending on the amount of time and whether you are staying there as a guest or not may mean you will incur a small fee for handling. Sending your parcel by Bussgods (Bus Cargo Shipping Sweden AB) may also be a cheaper option than by mail, depending on your original location. Check *http://www.bussgods.se/* and click on 'Send Packet' (*skicka paket*) for details.

The table below will assist you with your food and resupply planning. It indicates the availability of food stores and restaurants/cafés along the Kungsleden. It also includes the locations of postal services. Larger stores all stock gas and some replacement outdoor gear, should you require them during your thru-hike.

Location	Supermarket	Shop	Restaurant	Post Office/ Postal Box
Hemavan	√	√	√	√
Viterskalet		√		
Syter		√		
Tärnasjö		√		
Serve		√		
Aigert		√		
Ammarnäs	√	√	√	√
Bäverholmen		*limited	√	
Adolfström		√	√	√
Jäkkvik	√			√
Kvikkjokk		√	√	√
Aktse		√		
Saltoluokta		√	√	√
Vakkotavare		√		
Teusajaure		√		
Kaitumjaure		√		
Sälka		√		
Alesjaure		√		
Abiskojaure		√		
Abisko	√	√	√	√

(If an STF hut is not listed above, it indicates that it does not currently have a shop.)

Table 7 – Resupply Options in South-to-North Direction

[i] Fjällstations tend to offer an all-you-can-eat, buffet-style breakfast for around 85-95 SEK (£7-8) per person, which is a good option to set you up for the day, especially if you begin craving fresh food or are getting bored with your daily rations. It is a relatively inexpensive way of enjoying a hearty meal at regular intervals on the trail, which is a good motivating factor.

d. Training

The Kungsleden may be your greatest challenge to date, demanding more from you physically and mentally than any of your previous adventures. But fear not, with appropriate training, a solid foundation of physical fitness, and some mental fortitude you will make it across the finish line.

Mental Preparation

The right attitude in every phase of a long-distance hike is just as important as proper physical and logistical preparation. From the moment you make the decision, through the weeks of planning your trip, to the final day on the trail, maintaining an open mind and a resilient attitude in coping with obstacles is essential. At any given point, you may be confronted with fatigue, anxiety, or doubt. In those difficult moments, remind yourself why you chose to take on this challenge in the first place and that even the smallest steps in the right direction will help you achieve the goal eventually.

Physical Preparation

Endurance and strength are indispensable assets when it comes to going the full distance of a thru-hike. If your body is not used to walking long distances on a daily basis while carrying the extra weight of up to 18 kilograms (40 pounds), it will need proper conditioning. Individual workout needs may vary based on age, health, current fitness level, and other factors. However, the general intention is to get your body moving and comfortable with being active early on, and then gradually increase the intensity.

A good training routine will incorporate cardiovascular exercises and weight lifting elements. Go hiking frequently and participate in other forms of aerobic fitness, like cycling, swimming, running, or group fitness classes. This will not only increase your endurance, but also build confidence and momentum for your adventure. In addition, it is advisable to exercise with light to medium weights to strengthen shoulder and back muscles.

As your fitness level develops, it is crucial to add weight to some of your cardio exercises to simulate the backpack you will be carrying on the trail. Begin by wearing an empty pack, then a partially weighted pack, and eventually the equivalent weight of what you plan to carry during the trip. For an even better training effect, you could gradually progress your practice hikes to steeper terrain.

[**!**] The areas of your body most heavily stressed during the hike are your feet, shins, knees, back, and hips. If you've had problems with any of these parts in the past, it will be important to do some long training hikes to gauge and prepare for how your body will respond to the conditions on the Kungsleden, especially if you are intending on tackling the entire distance in one go.

Hiking Style

It is important to adopt a good hiking style in order for you to use your energy efficiently and to keep strains to your joints and tendons to a minimum. This includes hiking at a sustainable pace, taking small controlled steps, and placing your feet in the direction of the slope.

Hike at a Sustainable Pace

The Kungsleden is an ultra-ultra marathon, not a sprint. From an athletic perspective, this means that you need to keep your metabolism and energy conversion in an aerobic state. In brief, aerobic metabolism means that your muscles are receiving enough oxygen from your lungs, sufficient fuel through your bloodstream, and have enough time to dispose of by-products from burning the fuel, especially lactic acid.

The aerobic state or respiration is usually the sweet spot for your body to process its energy, from a nutritional intake as well as fat storage perspective. Keep in mind that even very fit people have an average body fat level of 5-15 percent. That means that a 72-kilogram (160 pounds) person would have around 7 kilograms (16 pounds) of fat, which contain approximately 56,000 calories – enough caloric energy for over 20 days. This body fat is a valuable reserve you should tap into on the trail in order to keep your packed food weight low and potentially reduce your body weight as a pleasant side effect. Maintaining a sustainable pace will allow you to do just that.

Your personal sustainable pace will vary depending on your level of fitness, the altitude, trail conditions, and even the temperature, among other factors. Finding your personal sustainable pace is simple. It is the pace at which you breathe deeply, but not rushed, you may sweat, but never excessively, and you feel you could hike like this for hours without having to stop for extended breaks frequently. As a result, a slow but sustainable pace will be the fastest way, because you will feel less fatigue and need less time to rest and recover.

Take Small Steps

Small steps can help reduce both the force of impact on your joints and the likelihood of a misstep or injury. The Kungsleden route has varying surface conditions. At times, you will have well placed steps on flat, well-trodden trails. Other times, you are walking along muddy woodland tracks, over boggy moorland or stony ground, which may cause stress on your feet. Taking small conscious steps keeps the strain on your muscles at a low level, avoiding muscle ache. Descending with a full pack can also result in knee, ankle, and shin pain. The larger the step, the greater the vertical drop and the greater the impact on your joints. Small steps are less likely to go wrong, as they have less momentum that could potentially cause you to twist your ankle or slip on loose gravel or other slippery surfaces.

Always Place Your Feet in the Direction of the Slope

This recommendation is especially important when hiking downhill. Look at the direction and angle of the slope. Always place your foot so that it is in line with the direction of the slope of the trail. If the path is going straight down the mountain, your toes should also point straight down. Why? Think of it this way, if you do slip, you want your toes to shoot forward so that you fall backwards. You may land on your bottom or your backpack, but both are padded. If you had your foot sideways and slipped, you could roll your ankle or land hard on your side.

Hiking with Trekking Poles

We prefer to walk with the assistance of trekking poles on any long-distance hike, as they provide more stability and balance when carrying a heavy pack and reduce the impact of hiking on legs, knees, ankles, and feet, meaning less stress on joints and muscles. On the Kungsleden, you will have to cross streams on stepping stones and traverse boggy moors. In such places, your poles are especially handy to test the solidity of the ground and to help keep you upright.

On steep ascents, trekking poles help hikers maintain forward momentum by recruiting upper body muscles to the task, reducing the strain that would ordinarily be absorbed by the lower body alone. This is particularly relevant when hiking up and over Tjäktja Pass, the highest point on the entire Kungsleden and most demanding climb. Walking with poles can also help you establish and maintain a consistent rhythm, which can reduce overall fatigue and increase your speed. This is especially true on flatter, non-technical terrain.

5. Gear

Choosing the right gear to take on a multi-day backpacking trip is an essential component to creating a memorable and pleasant experience. However, gear selection could easily be a separate book in itself. The following overview is intended to introduce the most commonly used items and provide Kungsleden-specific recommendations to aid your decision-making. Ultimately, what you need is gear that will keep you warm, dry, safe, and comfortable under any circumstances you can realistically expect to encounter on your journey.

a. Clothing

You will be faced with a wide variety of temperatures on the Kungsleden no matter when in the season you choose to hike the trail, ranging from moderately hot to very cold. Choosing efficient clothing is essential to keeping your pack weight down while enabling you to respond to the temperatures and extremes of weather you will likely encounter, regardless of the forecast, as it is always so changeable in the Swedish Arctic. Don't venture out onto the Kungsleden without appropriate attire to deal with rain and temperatures below freezing.

Clothing Basics

As a reminder, layering your clothing will maximise your comfort on the trail. This simple, proven concept allows you to make quick adjustments based on your activity level and potential changes in the weather. Each layer has a function. The base layer (against your skin) manages moisture, the middle layer provides insulation and protects you from the cold, and the shell layer (outer layer) shields you from wind and rain. Choosing your base, middle, and shell layers wisely will help control your body temperature in any condition and provide additional protection from the elements. You simply add or subtract layers as needed. Cotton fabrics should be avoided at all cost, since they absorb moisture quickly, take a long time to dry, and lose all their insulating properties when wet.

Daytime

Hiking in leggings/tights or lightweight hiking trousers and a long-sleeved technical base layer (lightweight, moisture-wicking, wool or synthetic material) over which a mid-weight insulating layer, such as a fleece or gilet, or wind jacket is worn, is perfectly adequate attire for most days on the

Kungsleden. If the temperature increases during the day, you can take off a layer or change into a short-sleeved T-shirt to feel more comfortable. As mosquitoes are prevalent during the summer months, it is not recommended to hike in shorts.

A heavier layer, such as a thick fleece or synthetic insulated jacket, may be needed for extra insulation on cooler mornings around camp and should definitely be carried for nighttime, when the temperature can drop dramatically. It is also important to carry a good, breathable waterproof jacket with hood and waterproof trousers, as rain is common in the summer and even snow can occur. Should the weather turn and temperatures fall, easy access points for these essential items are at the top of your pack or in front/side pouches, depending on the style of your backpack.

[i] If possible, opt for tops and jackets without seams on the shoulders to avoid rubbing and pressure points from your pack straps.

Another essential piece of kit is sun protection for your head and face in the form of a cap or a wide-brimmed hat. If you prefer to wear short-sleeved tops in hot weather, bear in mind the presence of mosquitoes and other biting insects and carry a repellent containing DEET, which is considered the most effective pesticide at deterring them. Also, use a sunscreen with a high SPF to adequately protect your skin from the sun.

Nighttime

In the evening, you may wish to change into something more comfortable, e.g., long trousers and a long-sleeved top different to that worn during the day. Alternatively, you could put on your sleepwear (thermal leggings and long-sleeved thermal top), thereby reducing the need for several sets of clothing. After setting up camp, if you are sitting around during the evening when the sun is less intense, you will need a warmer layer, such as a fleece jacket or an ultra-warm, compressible down jacket, to keep out the cold.

It is also important to have a warm hat, such as a beanie, thick gloves, and a multi-functional scarf (fleece-lined) as part of your clothing essentials kit to provide you with extra warmth at night. These are items that can make all the difference to your levels of comfort throughout the temperature ranges you will encounter on your trip.

A fleece or synthetic, insulated jacket may be more than adequate for a lot of people. However, as someone who sleeps 'cold', I wanted the extra warmth provided from a down jacket, which I also utilised as an additional layer in my sleeping bag during especially cold nights. I also carried down booties to keep my feet warm in the tent and when inside the mountain huts where you must remove your walking boots. In hindsight, an additional item I would like to have carried for nighttime are insulating down leggings, which would have been good for sitting around camp and to further boost the warmth of my sleeping bag.

Conventional down has three main benefits: it is ultralight, ultra-warm, and ultra-packable. However, is not the best material for damper climates, since it takes a long time to dry and won't insulate when wet. Because of the changing weather conditions along the Kungsleden, water-resistant down, synthetics, or down/synthetic hybrids perform better and are more practical. You should still try to prevent any clothing containing down from getting wet, so always remember to keep it in a dry sack inside your pack.

Additional Clothing

When considering underwear options, synthetic underwear is preferable as it is light, quick-drying, and has good breathability. You should avoid cotton as it doesn't wick moisture very well and is also known for chafing badly against the skin. Merino wool underwear is an excellent alternative, but is generally more expensive than synthetic materials.

When considering outer layers for your trip, a good quality mid-weight waterproof jacket (hard shell) will be suitable. This can also double up as a wind jacket. Good rain jackets will cost you money, but this an area where we feel your money will be well spent. You might find a cheaper jacket that will do the job, but if it decides to rain persistently over several hours, or days, you may regret choosing cost over performance. It's better to be confident about the reliability of your gear and not to have to worry about putting it to the test!

We would recommend on all hiking outings that you include a sun hat (cap, wide-brimmed hat) and cold weather head gear. You may also like to include a multifunctional scarf and ear warmers/ear muffs as part of your all-weather kit. These are really useful on cool mornings or evenings when you are sitting around camp.

Inside your sleeping bag, it is never advisable to sleep with your skin directly against the bag. Your choice of sleepwear is very personal, but your key priorities should be comfort and warmth. Our preferred choice of sleepwear is merino wool leggings and a long-sleeved merino top. We also add a CoolMax® liner to our kit. This is a polyester fabric which draws perspiration along its fibres away from the skin, used chiefly in sportswear. You can use a silk liner as an alternative. A liner protects your sleeping bag and gives you an extra layer of insulation, generally adding a couple of degrees to your bag.

It is a good idea to have an additional pair of shoes to wear around camp. Lightweight camp shoes, such as flip-flops or sports sandals, are really useful as changing out of your hiking boots, even for a short period of time, allows your feet to breathe and have a rest. They are also good for doubling up as footwear in public showers. We took lightweight sandals specifically as we were expecting to ford some streams along the route. However, bridges or stepping stones were in place at every crossing, so we never used our sandals for this purpose.

My preference as a woman is to hike in synthetic leggings (e.g., running compression leggings), which are really comfy to walk in. They are flexible and do not have a zip or button that can rub or become uncomfortable/bothersome whilst wearing a hip belt.

Washing Clothes

When considering your clothing options, keep in mind that the lighter your load, the more comfortable your walk. If you can double up on the function of anything, do so. Although, on the Kungsleden, there are few opportunities to wash and reuse items as proper laundry facilities are limited along the route. It may be possible to hand wash items and dry them in the STF huts that have specific drying rooms (*tork*), usually used by hikers for drying wet boots and waterproof gear. The Kvikkjokk Fjällstation does have a washing machine that you can use for a fee.

[!] Avoid contaminating natural water sources with soap when washing your clothes. Consider carrying a collapsible bucket and keep at least a distance of 60 metres (200 feet) from any stream or lake.

Sample Clothing List

This was our clothing packing list (each):

- 3 pairs of hiking socks
- 3 underwear
- 1 pair of bed socks or down booties
- 1 gilet (waistcoat)

- 1 short-sleeved T-shirt
- 1 down jacket
- 3 long-sleeved tops (incl. 1 sleepwear)
- 1 rain shell & trousers
- 3 leggings or hiking trousers (incl. 1 sleepwear)
- 1 cap & 1 woolly hat
- 1 mid-weight thermal jacket
- 1 pair of gloves

b. Hiking

Basic hiking gear usually consists of appropriate footwear, additional ankle and leg protection, a fitting and well-balanced backpack, and optional trekking poles. This section provides an overview of available options and features, discusses pros and cons, and offers advice on how to carefully choose and properly fit individual items.

Footwear

If you are going to be successful with walking 430 kilometres, then you need to carefully consider your choice of footwear, as it will be the most stressed piece of gear on your trip. Any good shoe has a thick, cushioning sole with non-slip tread. Beyond that, each of us has our own individual needs for footwear. A lot of which shoe or boot is right for you depends on how strong and flexible your ankles are, how much weight you plan on carrying, the size and shape of your feet, and the terrain you plan to cross, as well as just your preferences and what you feel most comfortable in. There are three typical styles – hiking boot, hiking shoe, and trail runner – that each have their individual assets and drawbacks. How suitable they are for the Kungsleden is considered below.

Hiking Boots

Hiking boots provide more stability overall and are the main choice of footwear for people hiking the Kungsleden. A well-fitting boot is snug, supports the ankle, and reduces the risk of twisting on a slight misstep. With more contact area, the foot can be less likely to move back and forth in a good boot. The high rising sides also offer ankle protection from hitting rocks and prevent grass seed and grit from entering the boot. Other advantages are warmth and water-resistance, which are of particular benefit on cold, rainy days in northern Sweden. Drawbacks of boots, especially the expensive, heavy, ankle-high leather hiking boots that many people wear on this trail, are the greater weight, stiffness (and hence resistance during walking strides), and lower breathability.

Hiking Shoes

Hiking shoes combine the grip stability of a good boot with more flexibility. The low cut allows more mobility and light mesh uppers enable moisture wicking. Lighter than boots, hiking shoes generally feel less restrictive while still providing sufficient stability. Watch out for firm heel support and a plastic cap to protect your toes. Different brands have various lacing systems, some enabling great fit in minimal time. There are a lot of benefits to hiking shoes, and they would be sufficient on the Kungsleden, as the trail is relatively flat and easy-going, if it wasn't for the unpredictable weather. Unfortunately, their drawbacks include reduced ankle support and reduced water-resistance. If you still decide this option is for you, hiking shoes lined with a waterproof membrane to help keep your feet dry, although making the shoe slightly heavier, is a better option for this walk.

Trail Runners

Trail runners go one step further regarding agility and lightness, weighing about as much as a conventional running shoe. Ultralight fell runners aiming to complete the Kungsleden in around a fortnight don this kind of footwear. However, it is not suitable for the average hiker on this trail. While still offering good tread and lots of grip, trail runners usually provide less cushioning than hiking shoes to save weight. Upper materials are mostly breathable, light meshes, offering more support than running shoes but far less than a boot. A further drawback is that the soles wear out much quicker when walking on hard surfaces, such as stony trails or tarmac. If you're covering 430 kilometres, you need to guarantee that your footwear will last, as replacing them on this trail is not an easy option!

Put your feet first! Whichever shoe or boot you decide to go with, make sure you are confident about your choice. It should provide adequate support to you and your pack weight, wick moisture from your feet, not be too heavy and tiring, have a well-cushioned sole, and, most importantly, a padded inside that does not cause blisters, as blisters can ruin even the best-laid walking plans.

[i] Feet swell during walking, so ensure your shoes are roomy. When shopping for new hiking shoes, wear the same type, thickness, and number of socks you'll be using when on the trail. If possible, try on new shoes at the end of the day, when your feet are puffed up to hiking size.

It is important that you never buy new hiking shoes just before you start a trip! We strongly recommend using your prospective shoes on at least a few training hikes to break them in and see how they perform. Walking as much as possible in your shoes will also help your skin to harden. If in doubt, try another pair.

For this trip, we chose lightweight hiking boots with a waterproof membrane and mid-cut profile as a compromise between a full hiking boot and hiking shoe. Hiking shoes are our usual preference for a long-distance hike. However, as we were concerned about keeping our feet as dry as possible, we adapted our gear for the conditions on the Kungsleden.

Whilst our hiking boots didn't keep our feet completely dry throughout the trip (even the most waterproof shoe reaches saturation point after several hours of continuous rain), we were happy with our decision on footwear. One of the benefits of lightweight, quick-drying material is that our boots soon dried out when put in the drying room for a few hours at an STF hut.

Gaiters, specifically designed to wrap around your lower leg or ankle and worn over your shoes, protecting the gap between sock and shoe from unwanted entrants, are another piece of gear that several hikers on the Kungsleden utilised, especially in wet weather on muddier sections of the trail. Whilst we have used gaiters in the past to perform this function and give added protection to our clothing, we did not include them as part of our pack list for this specific trip and do not consider them necessary. Instead, we preferred to put on waterproof trousers as an outer layer when needed.

Backpacks

Just like shoes, an ill-fitting backpack can cause considerable pain, which could be in the form of chafing along straps or back aches from a restrictive fit. When deciding on which backpack to use for your Kungsleden adventure, there are a multitude of styles, capacities, and functionalities to consider. This will include several elements, including size and overall capacity, actual weight, padding, adjustability, location of and how many compartments, ventilation, hydration system, and frame type.

From our own experience, many hikers along the Kungsleden trail seemed to have oversized packs with a large amount of equipment strapped to the pack externally as well. Although convenient, this could be problematic. For example, not having a large enough rain cover to go over both the backpack and equipment attached to the outside could result in wet gear. After talking with several hikers along the trail, most agreed they had brought too much stuff. Generally, the bigger your backpack, the more likely you are to fill it with extras. When deciding on the size of your backpack, one of the most important aspects to consider is how much weight you can comfortably carry. It is also important to stick to your packing list, especially if you are prone to overpacking!

Depending on your itinerary and preferred accommodation options along the Kungsleden, we would recommend the following capacity backpacks:

- Camping the entire way with all equipment included, you will need a large backpack of 50 litres or greater, depending on the size of your gear.

- Walking between mountain huts and mountain stations, or section hiking, whereby you don't need a tent, but you do need to provide your own sleep gear (e.g., sleeping bag, liner), then a pack of 30-40 litres should be adequate.

For our Kungsleden trip, we carried different-sized backpacks. Both lightweight packs with an internal aluminium frame, but Wayne's being slightly larger in capacity (65 litres) and weighing 2.2 kilograms (4.8 pounds), with a larger hip belt due to him carrying extra camera equipment and the tent. My backpack, a medium-sized 58-litre pack, weighed approximately 1 kilogram (2 pounds). Both packs were capable of carrying a decent load and were comfortable to wear. When full with supplies and equipment, my pack weighed in at 15 kilograms (33 pounds), with Wayne carrying the heavier load of 20 kilograms (44 pounds). Our packs were designed with similar features, including side pockets, front pouch, and removable top lid, providing easy access to all of our essentials.

[i] An important, if not essential, item to go with your backpack is a rain cover that attaches easily and quickly and fits well. If you intend on putting a lot of equipment in your side pockets or front pouch, it is worthwhile purchasing a larger cover to ensure that everything is well-protected from the elements, especially so on the Kungsleden.

Trekking Poles

Section 4d *Training* included some advice on the use of trekking poles. When used correctly, trekking poles do provide definite advantages, and we would not hike a long-distance trail without them. They are particularly beneficial on the Kungsleden, as they help you to move across the terrain quicker, especially important when you have a lot of miles to cover.

Here are some of the benefits:

- Increased stability in crossing streams on rocks/logs or wading.
- Increased stability while descending in mud/sand/loose gravel.
- Increased forward thrust and momentum.
- Reduced leg fatigue by recruiting upper body muscles.
- Reduced impact on legs/joints when descending slopes or steps.
- More effective rest while standing.
- Probe depth of water and firmness of snow.

Using hiking poles correctly is essential to unlocking their potential. Most poles will be adjustable in length, although some of the lower-end models as well as some ultralight models may be fixed in length.

We recommend that you use telescopic poles, as they have the additional benefit of being able to collapse down to a size that will make storing them easier when they are not in use. It is also advisable to carry spare tips, as we know from experience, replacing a broken tip on the trail is extremely difficult!

c. Sleeping

Getting better rest enhances every aspect of your camping experience and is crucial if you're to enjoy your long-distance hike. To ensure warmth, comfort, and dryness, which should be your main goals for a good night's sleep, you need an adequate sleeping system. Whilst for most hikers this will consist of a tent, sleeping bag, and sleep pad, there are some alternatives that you may wish to consider.

Shelters

When choosing a shelter, the decision comes down to how much weight you want to carry, how much money you want to spend, and how much protection you want from the elements. The pros and cons of the three most common shelter options (illustrated in Figure 30) are discussed below. If you are hiking with other people, you might consider sharing a shelter to save weight. However, this should be carefully weighed up against the benefits of having a separate shelter, which will offer a bit of privacy after a long day of hiking together.

| Single-Tent | Bivy | Tarp |

Figure 30 – Sleeping Shelter Options

Tent

Based on our own experience of the Kungsleden and the fact that rain is likely for a significant portion of your trip, the preferred shelter type was a two-skin tent, either tunnel- or dome-style. A tent provides the most space for you to dress and move around inside as well as for keeping your gear sheltered. Remember, not only rain but also condensation, especially in close proximity to lakes and rivers, will settle overnight and can soak your gear. If it does rain, is very windy, and/or you are cold, quickly pitching your tent and jumping inside provides instant protection and comfort. Getting food ready while taking a look at the map inside can be quite cosy, too. While the lightest single person tents are only around 1 kilogram (2 pounds), carrying a tent is the heaviest option for shelter.

As tents are usually made of rather thin fabrics to keep down the weight, adding a footprint to your setup might be a good idea. These durable, waterproof sheets are placed underneath the tent to protect the bottom from moisture and punctures.

[i] Tents have more surface area to collect moisture from rain and condensation, which will add weight to your pack. If you don't have time to let it air-dry, consider taking a small viscose sponge to wipe down any moist surface area before packing and hitting the trail.

Bivy

A bivouac sack, commonly known as *bivy*, is slightly bigger than a sleeping bag. The sleeping bag slides into the bivy, which is made of water- and wind-resistant material. A bivy sack has a small hole or breathable fabric in the head area which can either be left open or zipped shut. The head area generally also features a little dome, providing some extra space to rest on your elbows inside. While bivies offer similar insulation and protection from the elements as tents, inner condensation is a greater problem, because fabrics get in direct contact with the sleeping bag, resulting in reduced air circulation. Also, bivies offer no additional space for gear or extensive movement, and people with claustrophobia may not appreciate the confined space.

Under the Stars/Tarp

To anyone counting grams, a tent or even bivy might sound like a lot to carry. An alternative widely discussed in forums is sleeping under the stars as the night sky is spectacular. However, as there is a high chance it will rain at some point during your trip and because temperatures can fall below freezing during the night at higher elevations, using a tarp for camping in northern Sweden is not recommended. Likewise, tarps will rarely be as good a wind deflector or as insulating as a tent or bivy. So if you do choose this alternative, make sure your sleeping bag is adequate to combat the temperatures, including the wind-chill. A simple tarp may be the lightest and cheapest shelter but offers the least protection and privacy. It would definitely not suffice in persistent heavy rain, so you may find yourself seeking refuge in the nearest STF hut or emergency shelter!

In our opinion, neither a bivy nor a tarp are suitable for the wet weather or nighttime temperatures on the Kungsleden. We also didn't see anyone using these kinds of sleeping system. On our trip, we used a 3-season, 3-person, free standing, ultralight backpacking tent with separate fly and inner, weighing 1.8 kilograms (4 pounds), which offered us plenty of space as we were spending so much time in it. We appreciated the additional areas of dual vestibules, where we stored our packs at night. Other benefits of this particular tent are that it performed well in high winds and persistent rain and was both quick and easy to set up and pack away, especially in adverse weather conditions.

Sleeping Bags

Sleeping bags come in an overwhelming range of varieties depending on their primary purpose. It is all the more important to understand which features are essential for a multi-week backpacking adventure on the Kungsleden. A sleeping bag is a significant investment that should last for 10+ years if cared for properly. When choosing a model, there are three primary factors to consider: warmth, weight, and pack size.

Warmth

Warmth, expressed by the bag's temperature rating, will probably be the most important criteria in bag selection. Fortunately, there is an EN Standard[3] warmth measurement that lets you easily compare different models. Choose a bag with a temperature rating equal to or lower than the average monthly low temperature for wherever you will be camping.

On the Kungsleden, average daily lows in mid-summer only drop to around 9°C (48°F), so where the weather is mild, a 2-season sleeping bag with a temperature rating of +5°C will be sufficient. However, it is always better to opt for a lower comfort zone to be on the safe side, particularly as the weather is so unpredictable and temperatures can fall unexpectedly.

During September, as the hiking season comes to a close, average daily lows are around 4°C (39°F). However, at higher elevations it is common for temperatures to fall below freezing at night, so a 3- or 4-season sleeping bag may be more suitable depending on your personal preferences of sleeping hot or cold. A 1-season sleeping bag is ideal for indoor use, for example, when staying in a mountain hut or hostel.

For peace of mind, we recommend at least a 3-season sleeping bag for camping on the Kungsleden. This will have a comfort zone that is more than adequate for high summer, and if you find you are getting too hot, you can always unzip your bag and use it as a quilt or even sleep on top of it should nighttime temperatures remain in double figures.

[i] For additional warmth, consider a sleeping bag liner (made of silk, fleece, or synthetic materials), which can add 5-15 degrees to your bag. This will also help keeping your bag clean of dirt and body oils that can degrade its warmth over time.

---

3   EN Standard 13537: a European Standard (also used by some U.S. companies) for the testing, rating, and labelling of sleeping bags.

Peak performance sleeping bags use down insulation with fill-powers[4] of 700-900 or an equivalent synthetic composition. Down is breathable and provides an incredible loft and resulting insolation while being lightweight and compressing well. Additionally, there are new hydrophobic/dry downs that either repel moisture or maintain insulation properties even after getting wet. Modern synthetic fill materials mimic the great properties of down, often at a very competitive price. However, they are generally heavier and don't compress as well as down.

Weight

Weight is a general concern. Besides the filling, the weight is a function of length, girth, cut, fabric, and features of the sleeping bag. Length of the bag is usually a pretty clear decision based on your height. Girth will primarily be determined by your shoulders and belly or hips. Cut refers to the bag's shape. Most backpacking bags available today are mummy style that follows the contours of the body. Some bags are cut straight, providing more space but also more material to carry. Fabrics lining the sleeping bag are usually made of lightweight, synthetic materials. Features that enhance the bag's ability to retain heat include a drawstring hoodie to prevent heat loss from your head, a draft tube that covers the zipper to avoid heat loss on the side, and baffles or shingles that trap the down/synthetic fill in compartments to maintain even heat retention.

In order to reduce weight and bulk, many modern backpacking sleeping bags do not have padding on the side you will be lying on. There are two main reasons for this. First, the bag makers assume that most people will use a sleeping pad, which provides cushioning and insulation. Second, lying on the bag's insulation material compresses it, significantly reducing its effectiveness. Down-fill mummy bags will generally have the best warmth-to-weight ratios.

Pack Size

The amount of pack space a sleeping bag takes up is strongly correlated with its temperature rating, weight, and ultimately cost. Reducing the bag weight usually reduces the pack size, and more expensive bags will typically pack down to a smaller size. Warmer bags with more filling typically do not compress as much and will take up more pack space.

---

4   Fill-power: a measure of loft in cubic inches; it describes to what volume one ounce of down expands to.

Shelter Compatibility

Lastly, your choice of sleeping bag should match your choice of shelter. If you are sleeping with only a tarp or completely without a shelter, your sleeping bag should be especially warm, wind- and water-resistant. Keep in mind that water-resistant shells are less breathable and require more time for your bag to loft. If you plan to save weight on filling by wearing your jacket to sleep, make sure the sleeping bag provides enough inner space for the jacket's loft.

Taking all of these aspects into consideration, we chose an expensive, high-quality down sleeping bag that has a comfort rating of -2°C (28°F). Our decision was not based purely on hiking in Sweden. We have had the bags for three years now and have used them on several backpacking trips, including thru-hikes in England, the USA, South America, and other parts of Europe, so our final choice needed to meet several criteria. Again, it depends on your budget, but as we wanted a lightweight bag, we avoided heavy synthetic materials which are generally cheaper to purchase. Our down sleeping bags were a good choice for us in terms of both temperature and comfort. We always have an extra layer by way of a synthetic liner, and as I tend to sleep cold, I sometimes supplement my sleep gear by also wearing a down jacket.

[i] A sleeping bag doesn't warm your body, it merely traps the heat your body produces to allow you to remain warmer. If your body is exhausted and unable to produce proper warmth, you will remain cold regardless of the bag rating. To ensure against this, eat a robust, fatty meal just before bed to fuel your thermogenesis. Your body will generate more heat breaking down the fat than it will carbohydrates or sugar. Also remember to keep hydrated as being dehydrated leads to lower heat production.

Sleeping Pads

A good sleeping pads reduces heat loss through the ground, which maximizes your warmth, thereby supporting a good night's sleep. The two main criteria in your choice of sleeping pad are cushioning and insulation. Inflatable and closed-cell sleeping mats are most popular because of their comfort and weight. You can compare three equally-suitable alternatives below:

Air Pads – Similar to the ones used in swimming pools, camping air pads have a thin, air-tight shell that is inflated through a mouth valve. In order to cut down on weight, they are often semi-rectangular in shape. Air pads are very lightweight, roll up very small, and offer exceptional cushioning, especially those with a thickness of 5 centimetres (2 inches) and up. On the downside, inflating a thick pad may require more than a minute of lung blasting. Lightweight models can be noisy due to crackling material, and punctures are a concern. This type of pad is our preferred choice in terms of comfort. However, we have encountered several problems with regards to leaky valves, punctures, and chambers coming unstuck inside the pad, despite trying a couple of brands.

Foam Pads – Usually made of dense, closed-cell foams, foam pads can either be rolled up or folded like an accordion. Foam pads are lightweight, inexpensive, provide great insulation, and are practically indestructible from rough surfaces. On the downside, foam pads are usually not very thick and provide limited cushioning comfort. They also do not compress, hence packing rather large.

Self-inflating Foam Pads – Combining the packability of an air pad with the durability of a foam pad, while needing only little additional inflation. Thin pads are lightweight and compress well into a small sack. On the downside, they offer limited cushioning, while thicker pads of over 5 centimetres (2 inches) are very heavy.

[i] Whichever option you choose, make sure the pad is long enough and sufficiently wide at your shoulders. A good test is to lay on the pad in the shop before purchasing. For camping on the Kungsleden, a point to note is that your tent may at times be pitched on rough surfaces or low scrub that may threaten the integrity of your sleeping pad. It is advisable, therefore, to carry a small repair kit in case of a puncture.

Additional Comfort

Apart from the clothing you wear in your sleeping bag, there are other gear items that can provide additional comfort, such as a pillow, eye mask, ear plugs, and insect repellent.

[i] An alternative to packing an inflatable pillow is using your sleeping bag's stuff sack as a casing and stuffing it loosely with clothes.

An eye mask can be helpful to people with light-sensitive eyes, especially during the early summer months, when you will have almost 24 hours of daylight. You could use your scarf to make a blindfold by rolling it over your eyes. It might not seem comfortable at first, but it does make a difference. Ear plugs can be tricky, but if you cannot get any sleep due to surrounding noises, such as flowing rivers, they are useful. Insect repellent is another essential item for your comfort on the trail.

Unless you are hiking towards the end of the season, torches and/or headlamps are not so necessary on the Kungsleden as there is always enough light to see. Late August/early September, as the sun begins to dip earlier, you may need to use a headlamp for camp preparations in the evenings, early or late hiking, reading in the tent, and when nature calls at night. Headlamps are great because you have both hands free which is useful in any of the above scenarios (ensure adequate battery life). They are also useful at night inside the STF huts, as the only other source of light is candlelight which is not always sufficient for cooking.

d. Food & Water

Section 4b *Food* discussed options for meals along the Kungsleden, including what to bring and send as resupply, particularly as the majority of the time you will be camp cooking. This section focuses on the various gear items needed to store, prepare, and consume food as well as to treat and store water.

Stove & Fuel

If wild camping, the preparation of your meals will require a stove. Campfires cannot be relied upon in case of wet weather and lack of available/dry firewood. Camping stoves are much more convenient and efficient when it comes to timely meal preparation. They are light and reliable, while supporting the 'leave no trace' ethic. There are two common stove fuel systems – disposable gas cartridges and refillable liquid fuel canisters – that are almost certainly in stock at the few village stores you will pass on the Kungsleden. Likewise, STF huts with shops usually have a small selection of camping supplies. When deciding what system will work best for you, consider the factors below.

Cartridge stoves light instantly and give a full power flame from the word go. They pack up small, weigh very little, and hide away in your pan set until needed. They are cheap and simple, and the gas can be found in any camping shop. The gas cartridges don't leak and unscrew without hassle for packing. It is also safer to use in confined cooking areas, both due to a lower carbon monoxide poisoning risk and a more predicable flame (no priming flare-up).

A drawback to a cartridge stove, however, is that the gas it uses is too easily affected by cold and altitude. The canisters can become damaged or may be faulty, either through manufacturing flaw or through tampering. If the stove breaks, you can't often mend it. The heat output drops off as the cartridge loses pressure and can be painfully slow in bad weather.

Alternatively, liquid gas stoves are tough and dependable once mastered. They produce a consistent heat output in any condition, pumping out a constant flame that will not decrease as the fuel source empties. Although complex, they can be repaired in the field and many burn different types of fluid.

Disadvantages of carrying a liquid gas stove is that they are heavy, bulky, and overly complex. They can be dangerous due to flare-ups or fuel leaks and spills. They also become dirty and are bothersome to prime. They require patience and skill to use safely and effectively, especially as they can be poisonous in confined spaces. In addition, liquid gas stoves are considerably more expensive than cartridge models, the higher cost due to the increased complexity of design and construction.

Most people hiking the Kungsleden tend to use a cartridge stove system, as it is convenient for boiling water for hot drinks and adding to meals. Overall, however, they keep use of their stoves to a minimum by utilising the kitchen facilities provided by the STF huts.

We upgraded our cartridge stove for the purpose of this trip, as we wanted a lighter weight model that had a wind shield and functioned well within a low temperature range. We opted for a low profile, lightweight stove with inverted canister support and a hose connection. The big advantages of low profile, hose-connected stoves are stability and that they can be fully surrounded with a windshield (a foil one was provided with this stove), without fear of the canister overheating. The canister can be inverted to turn it from a gas to liquid feed in cold weather. It also has flip-out wire legs to support it. It's very easy to switch from an upright canister to an inverted one, and vice versa. We are confident of it working in below-freezing temperatures, which is perfect for the unpredictable Arctic. One morning on the Kungsleden, our canister was coated with frost. When lit in the upright position, the flame was sluggish, but as soon the canister was inverted, it roared into life.

Fuel Calculation

Another very important question is how much fuel to carry. If you don't have an STF membership and want to avoid paying to use the facilities of the huts, you will use more gas. Unless your meal plan requires special preparation, your fuel consumption will be directly proportioned to how much water you will need to boil per day. A good approximation of how much fuel is needed to boil water is 11.5 grams of fuel per litre of water (0.012 ounces of fuel per fluid ounce of water). If certain meals require simmering after the water has boiled, add 1 gram (0.035 ounces) of fuel per minute of cooking time.

Figure 31 below shows the equation used to estimate fuel consumption for the duration of your trip. Remember to include any side trips you plan on taking in your calculation. Once you know how much fuel you need, shop for a gas cartridge or fuel tank that will provide sufficient fuel while minimizing weight.

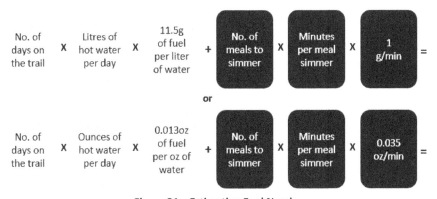

Figure 31 – Estimating Fuel Needs

Sample Scenario:

Anna is planning 26 days on the Kungsleden. Her estimates for hot water demand per day are as follows:

	235ml (8 oz.)	for coffee in the morning
+	235ml (8 oz.)	for porridge/oatmeal
+	0ml (0 oz.)	for lunch
+	470ml (16 oz.)	for a meal in the evening
+	235ml (8 oz.)	for one cup of tea
=	1.2l (40 oz.)	of boiling water per day

Ten of her meals each have to be simmered for 10 minutes. The rest of her meals are dehydrated/instant meals that do not require simmering. Consequently, her fuel estimate is as follows:

(26d x 1.2l x 11.5g/l) + (10d x 10min x 1g/min) = 459g

(26d x 40oz x 0.012oz/oz) + (10d x 10min x 0.035oz/min) = 16oz

So in total, Anna will need approximately 459 grams (16 ounces) of fuel for the entire trip. Gas canisters are generally available in three different volumes: 100g (3.5oz), 230g (8.1oz), and 450g (15.9oz). Anna can now decide if she wants to pack a large enough canister to last the entire trip duration or if she wants to pack a smaller cartridge first, then resupply or purchase extra fuel along the way, which will lighten her load.

[i] In order to keep boiling times and wasted fuel low, always use a lid, start on a small flame and increase as water gets warmer, never turning to full throttle. Furthermore, use a screen or heat reflector around your stove and pot to shield the flame from wind.

Lastly, don't forget to bring proper means to ignite a flame. Options include gas lighters, matches, piezo igniters, and spark strikers. Opt for something that is durable, long-lasting, reliable, and water-resistant. It is not recommended to solely rely on only one option. Bring at least one redundant option as a backup in case your first choice gets wet or breaks.

Water Treatment

As explained earlier in the book, on the Kungsleden, water can be taken directly from rivers and streams and safely drank without the need to purify it. It is so pristine and clear, you can drink it straight from the source. If, however, for peace of mind, you prefer to treat the water before drinking, there are several options for doing so. Micro-filter pumps, micro-filter gravity and squeeze bags, ultra-violet (UV) sterilization pens, chemical tablets/drops, and boiling are all options but can have their pros and cons.

Generally, filters treat protozoa, bacteria, and particles and allow instant water consumption. Boiling, UV light, and chemical purifiers are effective against protozoa, bacteria, and viruses, but only if the drawn water is almost clear and after a certain treatment time. All options except pumps are of limited applicability in shallow or small amounts of water.

Water Storage

Storage of large quantities of water is also not an issue on the Kungsleden. Most hikers carry plastic cups to take a drink from a passing river or stream whenever they are thirsty. They also carry a bottle or container for collecting water for cooking. As water availability is so regular on the trail, it means you can carry less and have a significantly lighter pack.

As we didn't bring or buy cups, we carried two 1-litre bottles each and found this was more than sufficient for keeping us hydrated while hiking. We refilled the bottles directly from flowing rivers or streams that had easy access down to the water's edge as we passed by or deliberately took a rest break if we wanted to top up our supplies prior to a lake crossing or beginning of a lengthy section where we wanted to cover a lot of ground without stopping. As we each also carried a water filter and a 2-litre pouch, sometimes late in the day, we filled up our pouches prior to setting up camp, so that we would have extra water for cooking or washing.

e. Medical & Personal Care

Your first aid kit is one of the few things that you will take on the Kungsleden but hopefully never have to use. Nonetheless, a well-equipped kit is vital in an emergency. In addition to bandages and antiseptics, your medical kit should include any personal medications you regularly take and anything that was recommended to you specifically for this trip. Make sure you know how to use all first aid materials you are taking with you. Otherwise, they won't be of any use if you get injured. Below are some materials that a good, basic first aid kit will include:

First Aid – General

- Self-adhesive bandages
- Tape (sufficient for emergency and blisters)
- Antibacterial wipes/ointment
- Non-stick sterile pads
- Self-adhesive elastic bandage wrap
- Scissors or knife
- Pain relieving gels/creams (with camphor, menthol, arnica)
- Anti-inflammatories and/or pain relievers (e.g., ibuprofen)

- Blister treatment (bandages, pads, etc.)
- Survival blanket (silver/insulated)
- Whistle

First Aid – Specific or Optional

- Any personal medication
- Antihistamines (to remedy allergic reactions)
- Tweezers (for splinters)
- Tick removal tool
- Safety pins
- Insect-sting relief
- Sun relief (e.g., aloe vera)
- Blood thinner (e.g., aspirin)

Personal Care

- Sunscreen (SPF 30 and up)
- Lip balm (with SPF)
- Toothbrush & paste
- Soap (biodegradable)
- Deodorant
- Insect repellent (suitable for mosquitoes)
- Moisturiser (sun cream can double up as this)
- Toilet paper (although most toilets at STF huts have both paper and sanitising gel)

f. Other Essentials

The following gear can be just as important as the gear listed earlier. Many choices are purely subject to personal preference. When deciding what other necessary items you are going to bring, remember that on a long-distance walk space is at a premium and that the main bulk of your pack's weight should be kept to essential items.

Gear	Comments
Camera	Consider the trade-off between weight and photo quality when deciding between DSLR, compact, and smartphone cameras. Ensure you have enough batteries and memory cards to meet the needs of your itinerary. On the Kungsleden, you will not find many options for charging gear. A camera clip that attaches to the shoulder strap of your backpack or a small padded (e.g., neoprene) case that attaches to your hip belt are conveniently accessible storage places for your camera. Likewise, a small dry bag attached to your pack with a carabiner clip works just as well.
Compass	Essential to have, especially when visibility is low.
GPS Watch	GPS watches, as used for running, show you exact distances travelled, speed, pace, elevation, etc. Software allows you to trace your every step back home at the computer and import data into online maps. They are good to have but not essential for navigating.
Light Source	Headlamps are a useful light source if you want to keep your hands free. Consider power-to-weight ratio as well as versatility. Carry a spare set of batteries, too.
Map/Map App	There are different map options available to purchase, showing the Kungsleden route, but the most up-to-date are the Calazo maps which are both light and compact. Options are discussed in more detail in Section 2a *Trails & Navigation*. Having a printed map is highly advisable, even if you plan on using an app. There are several map apps for Android and iOS, so check for recent releases. With your phone's GPS, the app can precisely locate your position on the trail. Some give additional information, e.g., elevation profile.
Money/ID	Bring sufficient cash to pay for accommodation, boat crossings, food, drinks, stove gas, post cards, emergency, etc. Towns and larger villages have the facility to pay by card, as do all Fjällstations and some mountain huts en route. But do not rely on this method of payment.
Rope	Useful to hang clothes, replace a strap on a backpack, or as a shoe lace. It should not be too thick or heavy. 5 metres (16 feet) is a good length. Examples: paracord, dyneema cord.

Satellite Communicator (optional)	Beyond the reliable range of cell phones, there are three types of satellite communicators that can make or maintain contact with family, friends, and emergency response teams: • Personal locator beacons (PLB) • Satellite phones • Satellite messengers These devices can share additional details in the event of an emergency (e.g., location, type of injury, patient information), which improves the efficiency of search and rescue efforts. Consider carrying a satellite communicator if you are diverting off the Kungsleden into areas with unmarked trails, such as Sarek National Park.
Solar Charger (optional)	Very much dependent on how many electronic devices you are intending to carry and where you plan to sleep. A variety of compact photovoltaic panels incl. rechargeable battery and USB power port are available. Make sure you have enough power if you plan to carry several devices (light, smartphone, GPS watch, etc.).
Sunglasses	Sporty, tight fit, UV protection, polarisation is a plus.
Pack of Tissues	Keep a small pack of tissues, a small bottle of hand sanitiser, and a small pack of wet wipes in your top lid for emergencies.
Towel	Quick drying, synthetic fabric, lightweight.
Trowel (optional)	Useful to bury human waste. Should be light but sturdy as the ground can be rocky and tough. A walking pole can double up for this function. Pit toilets are often available along the way.
Sewing Kit & Duct Tape	Make sure your kit contains essentials for outdoor repairs, e.g., heavy duty thread, strong needle. Or bring 1 large-eyed needle to easily thread dental floss, so it can have a dual purpose. Alternatively, duct tape fixes almost anything! Wrap some around your trekking poles for an emergency repair.

Table 8 – Other Essential Gear

6. Personal Experience

This chapter describes our personal preparations, travel arrangements, gear items, and experience on the Kungsleden. It is a summary of considerations and efforts that went into our own 21-day journey in August/September 2016 and exemplifies what worked for us as a hiking couple. The below information is intended to provide inspiration, additional guidance, and reference points for shaping your own trip.

a. Plan

Long Lead Items

Having completed some of the world's best known long-distance hikes over the last few years, we decided that for our next adventure we wanted to choose a place that would present us with new experiences on the trail. Having had a tough summer the previous year completing the GR20 across Corsica, we very much wanted a walking trail, as opposed to a scrambling route, and decided that the Kungsleden ticked all the right boxes for us! Neither of us had visited Sweden before nor hiked in northern Europe, so as Sweden's 'King of Trails', the Kungsleden promised incredible mountain scenery as well as the unique element that we'd be venturing into the Arctic Circle for the very first time.

At the initial stages, we researched what a Kungsleden thru-hike would entail and read several blogs detailing other hikers' day-to-day experiences, as we found a limited supply of guidebooks written in English. Drawing knowledge from other people's first-hand experiences on the trail is an invaluable tool to get straight to the heart of whether the trail is for you or not. Then, we put together an achievable itinerary based on our capabilities from previous hikes. What really appealed to us about the Kungsleden was that we wouldn't have to carry several days' worth of food rations in one go, as we could resupply regularly along the trail. If we were faced with severe weather, the STF huts would provide a good backup.

With me being a primary school teacher, we were restricted to school holiday dates. Although usually prudent to avoid the peak time of July/August when hiking in England, it is different in Sweden, as this is high summer on the Kungsleden and the best time to go in terms of the weather and daylight hours – but not so if you want to avoid the mosquitoes. As we really wanted to minimise annoyances from these biting pests, we opted for an August start, with a completion in early September. We booked our flights as soon as they went on sale for that period to secure our preferred dates and the best price. (This was 8 months in advance!) We took an early morning flight from London Gatwick to Stockholm, which is a convenient 2.5-hour journey. Then, from Stockholm, we took an internal flight to Hemavan, arriving at 9:00 PM the same day.

Having a confirmed start and end date, we booked accommodation in Hemavan, as we knew we would be arriving late and not setting off on the trail until the following day. Plus, we pre-booked accommodation for our finish date in Abisko, as we knew we would want some home comforts after twenty nights on the trail. We also booked tickets for the overnight train back to Stockholm prior to our return flight home to secure a sleeper compartment, which saved us money on an extra night's accommodation.

Itinerary

After our initial research, we had already decided that we'd walk the Kungsleden in the very unconventional direction of south to north, largely to avoid the Fjällräven Classic, which would be taking place during our trip. We also wanted to avoid walking with the sun in our faces and were under the impression that we would be saving the best until last! So decision made, we set about breaking the route up into manageable walking distances and noted the locations of the STF huts along the route. We kept a table of this information on our smartphones for future reference. Usually, we would also consider good places to camp at this point. However, as Sweden permits wild camping virtually anywhere and water sources are frequent, we didn't see the need to plan this in any detail. We just looked at our maps for locations of lakes and any spots we thought might be particularly scenic and made a note of them.

Having had the 'Skierfe Detour' recommended to us, we knew we wanted to allow at least a half day to get to the lookout point on the eastern border of Sarek National Park. We were also considering an ascent of Kebnekaise, but this would be very weather-dependent. We knew it would require at least two extra days, which may have been time we wouldn't have if weather hampered our progress early on in the south. So we left this option open and agreed that we would make the decision on the trail according to conditions. Plus, we would need to divide the distance that was remaining to Abisko with how many days we had left after reaching Singi, the point at which you can turn off the trail and head to Kebnekaise mountain station, to see whether diverting to Kebnekaise and still getting to Abisko on time would be achievable.

Having adjusted it on the go in light of what was discussed above, a table showing our actual day-by-day itinerary is included below:

Campsite	Day	Distance (km)	Total Dist. (km)	Elevation (m)	Elevation Gain (m)	Elevation Loss (m)
Hemavan	-	-	-	530	-	-
Syter +2km	1	25.5	25.5	743	582	521
Tärnasjö Hut	2	12.4	37.9	612	60	102
Vuomatjåhkka +3km	3	23.2	61.1	839	468	408
Ammarnäs +5km	4	25.1	86.2	454	411	532
Sjnulttjie Shelter	5	29.2	115.4	746	639	574
Adolfström	6	23.7	139.1	483	326	393
Jäkkvik	7	21.7	160.8	441	589	604
Vuonatjviken +2.5km	8	26.8	197.6	585	363	318
Tjaurakatan (near)	9	18.9	206.5	787	130	101
Suonergarssa	10	25.8	232.3	786	127	231
Kvikkjokk	11	22.1	254.4	332	248	388
Pårte +4km	12	19.7	274.1	613	293	249
Skierfe Detour (1km from trail)	13	23.8	297.9	806	379	372
Sitojaure +5km	14	28.2	326.1	805	431	447
Saltoluokta	15	14.8	340.9	428	146	262
Teusajaure	16	44.9*	385.8*	496	174	153
Singi -1km	17	21.1	406.9	701	105	86
Tjäktjastuga +1km	18	26.4	433.3	991	474	391
Alesjaure	19	12.7	446	806	170	244
Nissonjokk	20	31.2	477.2	403	199	321
Abisko	21	4.4	481.6	318	93	114

*(includes 30km by bus)

Table 9 – Personal 21-Day Itinerary

As you can see, we didn't include Kebnekaise in our own Kungsleden thru-hike as the weather in the north was so changeable when we got to that section. We also adjusted our itinerary to leave us just 4 kilometres or so to reach Abisko on our final hiking day so that we would have more time to spend in Abisko and enjoy the facilities at our hostel.

Food & Resupply

If your itinerary involves camping and cooking your own meals, food and nutrition will play a major role in your planning and preparation. In addition to the suggestions in Section 4b *Food*, here are some personal remarks on the food we brought.

In general, we like to carry enough food to keep us going for two to three days, as well as a set of emergency rations kept at the bottom of our packs. This always ensures that we have adequate provisions should the location of shop facilities be particularly sparse along certain sections of the route or if our intended arrival time does not coincide with opening hours. As stated previously, it is not really necessary to carry several days' worth of food with you or send yourself resupply packages, as you can resupply almost daily along the way. Although you will need to budget appropriately for this as it is the most expensive option.

We brought with us a few supplies from the UK that we thought may be difficult to acquire in Sweden, such as milk powder, tea bags, packet soup, individual portions of hot chocolate, and cured sausage. However, we found all of these items available along the trail in the larger STF shops.

In Hemavan, prior to starting the trail, we stocked up with food rations for the first few days as there is a large supermarket with a full range of goods. Similarly, we resupplied from the supermarkets in Ammarnäs and Jäkkvik as there is a wider range of hiker food and it is cheaper than purchasing food stuffs in the STF mountain hut shops. Further resupply was done at the STF Kvikkjokk and Saltoluokta mountain stations, as their shops are bigger with more variety. Having acquired the basics for meals, we then topped up our snacks at the mountain huts as we went along the trail.

Meal	Comments
Breakfast	Our standard breakfast was an individual portion of muesli and dried fruit combined with milk powder, mixed with cold water, and a cup of tea. If it was a particularly cold morning, we would have hot soup instead, made with a packet of dry soup mix and boiling water. Our strategy was to get dressed and empty the tent, then boil water while we finished breaking camp and packing. That way, we could eat a simple breakfast and hit the trail quickly, knowing that we had packed plenty of snacks to fuel us throughout the day.
Lunch	Tinned mackerel with bread rolls or crackers, a packet of dry soup mix and boiling water, or shared snacks on the go, such as packets of crisps, crackers, peanuts, or biscuits.

Snacks	Our snacks were nuts, crackers, crisps, and bags of jelly sweets, and we always ate at least one large chocolate bar per day. If fresh fruit was available, we would buy bananas or oranges. We always made sure to eat something on our arrival into camp to avoid crashing before getting the camp chores done and making dinner. An afternoon tea or hot chocolate in camp was always a welcome treat.
Dinner	We opted for convenience and ease of clean-up for our dinners and mostly avoided purchasing tinned foods, unless we were close to an STF hut to clean and dispose of rubbish in recycling bins. Our main food stuffs included instant noodles, instant mashed potatoes, pasta, or rice for extra nourishment on our longer trail days. We used packet sauces and carried salami, cheese, and small tins of fish for protein and extra flavour. Meatballs and goulash were treats when camping next to an STF hut.

Table 10 – Personal Food Strategy & Comments

Along with our food rations, we also carry salt, pepper, and spices, such as chilli and curry powder, as well as two mini bottles of olive oil to aid with cooking. You may consider these items a luxury, but they really helped to make the food we were eating flavoursome and appealing.

Our food rations and meal ideas worked well and suited us, not least because Wayne is a really good cook and can turn anything remotely 'instant' into something mouth-wateringly good. We both had defined camp roles – Wayne being the 'chef' and I being the 'washer-upper'. We did supplement our camp meals with three all-you-can-eat, buffet-style breakfasts, available for less than 100 SEK (£9) p/p at mountain station restaurants. They were worth every penny, as they really set us up for the day and satiated our craving for fresh food after a few days of wild camping and eating instant food made with boiling water.

We didn't have anything special for carrying our food. After purchasing, we generally divvied it up by weight so that both of us carried a similar amount on top of the gear already in our packs. I kept mine together in a carrier bag towards the top of my pack for easy access, whereas Wayne split his rations up, putting food in various compartments so that his pack was equally balanced. We tended to keep the food in a dry bag at night inside our tent and never had any problems with wildlife searching out the food unlike on other long-distance hikes we've completed.

Training

As we considered ourselves reasonably fit and often went on weekend walking trips, we didn't devise a training schedule prior to this long-distance hike, despite doing this in the past and finding it very beneficial. Incorporating day walks of around 16 kilometres (10 miles) in and around our local area, gradually building up to between 24 and 32 kilometres (15-20 miles) of walking per day, has previously helped our bodies get accustomed to carrying a heavier pack. We believe this ensures a greater chance of success for completing a thru-hike. But as the Kungsleden promised relatively good walking trails on easy terrain with only modest height gains and losses over the course of the route, we were not overly concerned with the length of the trail. As long as we would complete on time, the rest of our itinerary had some flexibility, i.e., daily distances could be adjusted according to how we felt on a particular day, what the weather was like, and how difficult it was navigating the terrain.

Gear

Being born and bred in England, we were used to experiencing cold, wet weather whilst hiking, so we knew what to expect in terms of the weather on the Kungsleden. As we used much of the same kit from our previous long-distance hikes, all of our gear was tried and tested for performance, durability, and comfort in different weather conditions, so we were confident it would prove reliable in Sweden, too. The only thing we specifically upgraded to reduce weight and provide us with a higher level of comfort for this trip was our tent.

Figure 32 – Gear Selection prior to Trip | Packed Backpacks and Must-Have Walking Poles

Our general attitude towards gear is that you get what you pay for, so if you want gear of good quality that will stand the test of time, it is worth investing in and spending that little bit more. If you are hiking over a long distance, then the weight you are carrying is of significant importance. Lightweight gear options are therefore preferable, but these tend to be more expensive, so your budget will determine how lightweight you can actually go. A thorough scrutinising of your intended kit list is a good idea so that you can try and reduce your pack weight by discarding any unnecessary items (something we still need to get better at!).

As we anticipated cold, wet weather on the Kungsleden, we planned our gear accordingly. Below is an overview of our equipment along with some comments:

Gear Item	Comments
Backpack	We carried different-sized lightweight packs with an internal aluminium frame: • 65-litre capacity, not the lightest model (2.2kg/4.8lbs) but very durable, well-padded, and ventilated, with a larger hip belt due to extra camera equipment and tent. • 58-litre capacity (1kg/2lbs), capable of carrying a decent load due to frame and comfortable to wear. When full with supplies and equipment, my pack weighed in at 15kg (33lbs), with Wayne carrying the heavier load of 20kg (44lbs). Our packs were designed with similar features, including side pockets, front pouch, and removable top lid, providing easy access to all of our essentials.
Trekking poles	As stated earlier, the use of trekking poles is highly recommended. We used 3-section telescoping poles with an external lever lock style mechanism and foam grips (390g per pair). These had served us very well on previous trips and on the Kungsleden. However, Wayne snapped his pole by getting it caught between two rocks mid-way through the trip and had to do a make-shift repair on the trail. We recommend investing a little more in higher quality poles, especially if you plan to double them as tent poles.
Shelter	3-person, 3-season, free-standing, ultralight tent with separate fly and inner without footprint (packed weight approx. 1.8kg/4lbs). The extra weight is nothing compared to the additional comfort and moving space. We also appreciated the additional areas of dual vestibules, where we stored our packs at night.
Sleeping pad	Ultralight, 4-season, inflatable pad with microfibre insulation and 9cm (3.5 inches) thickness in a tapered design. We upgraded our sleep pads to provide more comfort in colder conditions. At 405g each, they are well worth the cost.

Sleeping bag	800-fill duck down bags with a comfort rating of 2.5°C (36.5°F) and a limit of -3°C (26.5°F). With a pack weight of 850g (2 lbs.), it's not quite the ultralight option but very comfortable and warm. Comfort zones of 0-5°C (32-40°F) may work as well, but I wouldn't go any higher than that. We found that these bags were just about adequate for the Swedish summer climate with the addition of a liner. On particularly cold nights, I would also wear a down jacket inside the bag to provide extra warmth.
Stove & fuel	Simple, low profile, lightweight 3-arm-foldout stove with inverted canister support and a hose connection. It had a wind shield and functioned well within a low temperature range. Gas cartridge with isobutane mix – easy handling, worked great. We used about two 230g (8.1oz) canisters during our trip.
Cookware & utensils	Two-person cook set, including two bowls, two cups, aluminium cooking pot with a capacity of 1.1l with fold-up side handle and lid. Also, two sporks, an outdoor knife (for slicing up food), and a long metal spoon (for stirring food in a tall pot).
Water treatment	While not required on the Kungsleden, we took a squeeze filter system that comprises of a filter unit, squeeze pouch, and small syringe for cleaning. We just used the pouch to collect extra water for cooking.
Hydration system	We didn't carry a hydration pack. Having previously used them in South America, we found them cumbersome in our backpacks. We each carried two standard 1-litre water bottles that we refilled from flowing water sources along the trail whenever needed.
Camera	Being keen photographers, cameras are an essential part of our kit. We both carried compact system cameras with 9-18mm & 25mm lenses, 5 x 32GB SD cards, and 3 extra camera batteries, plus lightweight tripod, portable flexible tripod, and a small, waterproof action camera on a selfie stick. Wayne also carried a high-end drone to film the trail, with 2 extra batteries and charger. The batteries didn't work in the mornings when it was too cold. As a tip, try to keep them in/near your sleeping bag or carry the battery separately in a pant pocket in the morning for quicker warming up. We also have aluminium clips to attach our cameras directly to a backpack strap so that we have easy access to a camera at all times. We would highly recommend this approach.
GPS Watch	Not worn, but GPS was accessed via smartphone. This would be a good addition to our kit to save on battery power.
Satellite communicator	We didn't carry one on this trip, but it is a highly recommended piece of kit, especially if you are hiking alone.
Solar charger	460g compact and efficient solar panel with two USB outputs, ideal for charging smartphones on the go.

Map/map app	We used the Swedish 1:100,000 maps produced by Calazo. The 4 maps weigh a total of 140g, are compact in size, and the format is easy to follow. In addition, we used the ViewRanger app for android smartphone loaded with the map set.
Light source	Battery-powered headlamps which were only really used during the last few nights of our trip as sunset got earlier. We also packed a small battery pack with a USB port that connected to an LED light built into our tent.
Battery pack	13000mAh capacity. It can recharge a smartphone over six times. It has dual USB outputs (1A and 2A) and can charge compact cameras in addition to smartphones.

Table 11 – Personal Gear List & Comments

Additional Tips

For some, ultralight backpacking is the key to a successful thru-hike. For us, it's a balance between weight versus comfort, whilst having gear that is both reliable and durable. Compromises may have to be made due to budget limitations, but we believe items such as sleep system, footwear, and waterproof layers are always worth investing in and spending that bit extra on. Reliable gear makes for a much more enjoyable hike!

b. Go

Day 1: Hemavan to Wild Camp (2km past Syter STF Hut)

Distance:	25.5 km/15.9 miles	Elev. Gain/Loss (m):	+582/-521
Duration:	10 hours	Difficulty Level:	moderate

What a start! After an incredibly scenic flight into Hemavan the day before, we woke up to light rain. It didn't bode well for our first day on the trail. We decided a hearty, all-you-can-eat-style breakfast at our hostel, the Hemavans Fjällcenter, would set us up for the day. It was to be our first day of hiking with heavy packs in around a year, so we needed all the energy we could get. It turned out to be the best breakfast selection we had on the entire trail, and it was the best value for the money at 85 SEK (£7.50) p/p. We thoroughly recommend it whether it be at the start or end of your own Kungsleden adventure!

Feeling very full, we walked into town at 9:00 AM. Our mission was to purchase food rations for the next few days. We also needed to post on our hand luggage (containing anything we didn't need for the hike) to the hostel in Abisko, which we had pre-booked in anticipation of our finish on

September 2nd. We spent 250 SEK (£22) in the supermarket on 2 day's hiking rations. Additionally, we purchased gas for our camp stove from a hiking gear/cycle shop next to the hostel. After packing our new supplies, we set off to find the official start of the trail at 10:30 AM. Of course, we had to get a photo at the large, wooden Kungsleden trail sign, right next to the Vindelfjällen Nature Reserve visitor centre. And so our Kungsleden journey began – in full waterproofs, which we seemed to wear more often than not!

Figure 33 – Start of the Trail in Hemavan| Wet Weather and Boggy Trail

Our aim for the day was to camp just beyond the Syterstugan hut. We found the trail to be well-trodden, making it both clear and easy to follow. However, several sections were very boggy, so we were grateful of the provision of wooden boardwalks along the route where the trail went straight through it. We were already getting a sense of the Kungsleden's reputation as wild and remote, and the valley we were walking through would have been an incredibly scenic start, had it not been for the persistent rain clouds looming overhead the entire day.

We stopped at the Viter STF hut for a rest break and, after looking around at all of the facilities, we were immensely impressed with the setup. We felt very civilised (and very English), having a cup of tea with biscuits, whilst we refreshed ourselves and dried out a bit, thankful of the large wood burning stove in the kitchen area that warmed us through as soon as we entered the cosy space. Having hardly seen a soul on the trail from the moment we got started, we were surprised that the hut was very busy with hikers using it as lodging for the night. Well, why not?! It was so well-equipped with everything that, if you didn't want to carry a tent or cooking equipment, you could make the hike much easier for yourself by overnighting in each hut. (You would just need a lot of money to do so!)

Figure 34 – Dubious Looking Bridge over Rocky Stream | Viter STF Hut

After warming up and drying out a little, we had to motivate ourselves to get the packs back on and get going again, as we weren't even halfway to our intended camp spot. From then on, we walked in persistent light rain that got a little worse in the last hour before reaching camp, which meant our waterproof boots had eventually reached saturation point and had started leaching in water. Humongous snow-capped mountains loomed either side, and we felt we were heading further and further away from civilisation into the wilds of northern Sweden. The one thing we didn't have to worry too much about was daylight, with it still easily being light until around 11:00 PM.

By the time we had pitched our tent and done the most important tasks of the day – cooking and eating dinner – it was nearing 10:30 PM! It had seemed a long day but still wasn't dark, yet (which felt quite strange). The rain was heavier than ever, so we were glad our new shelter was proving its worth and keeping us dry. We hoped the weather would significantly improve tomorrow, especially as we couldn't bear to think of 20 repeats of today. However, we both agreed on the one consolation of a rainy day – no mosquitoes!

Day 2: Wild Camp (2km past Syter Hut) to Tärnasjö STF Hut

Distance:	12.4 km/7.7 miles	Elev. Gain/Loss (m):	+60/-102
Duration:	5 hours	Difficulty Level:	moderate

After yesterday's mammoth 10 hours of walking, we decided to stay put in the tent and have a little lie-in, in the hope that there'd be a break in the rain long enough to pack the tent away without us getting soaked before we had even set off. Thankfully, by 11:00 AM the rain had slowed into a fine drizzle, with our direction of travel looking brighter and more promising.

Today involved circumnavigating lots of water, which was helped with several bridge crossings, as we made our way north alongside Lake Tärnasjö. What also lightened our spirits was speaking to an Aussie guy, who was hiking in the opposite direction. He was a lot wetter than us and was intending on pushing through to Hemavan and completing the trail today, having hiked the entire route from north to south. Regaling us with tales from the northern section, he made us even more excited and determined to get there, confirming that the beauty and spectacular scenery of the north far outweighs that of the southern section.

Figure 35 – Crossing Waterlogged Sections on Boardwalks| Heading Around the Lake

However, the valley we hiked through yesterday begged to differ. Both grand and impressive, if it hadn't been for such dreadful weather, it would have been a spectacular walk indeed. We commented that the craggy mountains and rolling hills carpeted in light green were just like those of the western lakeland fells back home, except that everywhere you looked, it was on a much larger, grander scale. The valleys were vaster, the mountains were more immense. Basically, it was the Lake District on steroids!

After leaving our wild camp spot, the trail headed lakeside, causing us significant stress to our feet and ankles, as we had to pick our way over undulating rocks and roots, whilst also contending with thick, suffocating mud. It was both burdensome and tiringly long, although technically on paper, we'd only hiked a few miles. We couldn't be growing weary of the trail already as we had hardly got anywhere!

It was the seemingly endless 4-kilometre stretch to the Tärnasjö STF mountain hut that made our minds up. We decided to cut the day short and camp there for the night. After purchasing a tin of Swedish meatballs from the on-site shop for dinner that evening, we went off to experience another truly Swedish phenomenon – the sauna.

We never envisaged that on the second day of our journey on the Kungsleden, we'd be bailing out early to sit naked with a group of strangers in a little, wooden room heated to nearly 100°C (212°F)! (Well, almost naked...) As newcomers to the Swedish sauna, we weren't quite brave enough to bare everything the first time round. But this taster session certainly provided an insight into the Swedish psyche, where nudity is completely normal and natural, making us reserved Brits feel very prudish indeed. It also enabled us to get properly acquainted with sauna etiquette and ready for our second visit, where we did bare all, as we were assured that sweating away life's problems in a baking-hot sauna is an essential part of the Swedish experience!

We had to quickly get comfortable in our own skin and overcome that initial 'awkwardness' of knowing where to focus your eyes. But once you let go of your own hang-ups, you can really enjoy the sauna for what it is – the perfect place to relieve a bit of stress and tension and revive your aching muscles. We found the experience to be both wonderfully relaxing and super-liberating, plus a little crazy. This is in reference to the bit where you then go outside (still naked) and run into the lake to refresh yourself in the freezing water. (We were told that in winter you roll in the snow instead!) No wonder the Swedes incorporate saunas into their daily lives and have installed them, together with the mountain huts, along the 430-kilometre Kungsleden! We couldn't wait to reach the next one!

Figure 36 – Sauna next to Lake Tärnasjö | Using Mountain Hut Facilities

Afterwards, I set about washing our essentials in a bowl of hot water (taken from the sauna). I stood at the lakeside by the jetty, but this turned out to be a huge mistake, as I was attacked by a fervent cloud of biting gnats. They were both annoying and unstoppable, no matter what avoidance tactic I used. I tried to cover every bit of bare flesh possible, but the only real respite I got was back in the tent when the job was finished. Later that evening, we sat inside the hut and used the kitchen facilities for preparing dinner. Not only were we newcomers to the sauna, but it was our first time trying Swedish meatballs from a tin as well. Enjoying dinner by candlelight, it didn't feel like we were roughing it on this trail with the excellent facilities of the mountain huts!

Day 3: Tärnasjö STF Hut to Wild Camp (Vuomatjåhkka +3km)

Distance:	23.2 km/14.4 miles	Elev. Gain/Loss (m):	+468/-408
Duration:	10 hours	Difficulty Level:	moderate

After yesterday's unique sauna experience, we had a great night's sleep. In fact, we both slept like logs and woke up feeling really refreshed and ready to face a new day, whatever the weather would bring. But instead of hitting the trail and putting our renewed energy to immediate use, we thought we might as well make use of the hut's facilities one last time.

Having already been introduced to the effective operational procedures of the mountain hut system, where everyone is expected to do their bit, we dutifully refilled the fresh water buckets, disposed of any waste water in the *slask* and sorted out our rubbish into the correct recycling bins before bidding farewell to what had been a cosy, little retreat. Back on the trail, we were reliving last night's events, firm in the opinion that we'd most definitely be camping at the next mountain hut we came across that was located beside a lake, making full use of the facilities again. Because of the rain, the sauna had been our best experience on the Kungsleden so far! But all of that was about to change...

Figure 37 – Well-Defined Trail | Enjoying the View from a Footbridge

Not only was the weather much more forgiving, the landscape, too, was both vast and varied but remarkably flat, making for a much easier day's walk. When you think of the Arctic Circle, what comes to mind is one of the harshest environments on our planet, where little can survive. Yet, the Kungsleden was taking us across miles upon miles of vibrant green wide-open land, richly covered in a variety of flora. From the striking purple thistle that reminded us of roaming the Scottish highlands, to moors filled with golden yellow buttercups, to Sweden's tiny national treasure – the prized cloudberry, growing in waterlogged ground. The open fells were abundantly alive and beginning to show the first signs of autumn.

We took a slow and steady walk up a gentle hill that was carpeted in wild blueberries. From the highest point, we had a full 360-degree view of the surrounding valley, so we decided that this would be a perfect spot to get the drone out and fly it for the first time on the trail. Whilst Wayne then set up some different shots, I busied myself with trying to find the biggest and most ripe blueberries, picking a bag full of them to enjoy as a snack for later.

Figure 38 – Rest Break to Take In the Scenery | Wild Camp Spot at Sunset

As we continued along the trail, the horizon was lined with impressive peaks. Although it was a long day of hiking, the trail wasn't too taxing, the route over the lower fells taking us on a well-defined footpath. However, it was clear that we had greatly overestimated how far we would walk today. Our initial plan to reach Ammarnäs by the end of day 3 was just way too unrealistic, so we decided on aiming for halfway to Ammarnäs instead – or as near as we could push ourselves. Despite changing our plans, it was still 17 kilometres to the Aigert mountain hut, located at the foot of Mount Äijvisåive, a holy mountain for the Sámi people, so we knew, we wouldn't make it that far either.

Instead, we decided that we'd camp close to one of the emergency shelters that we'd be passing within the next hour or so, as we wanted to set up camp before the sun dipped behind the mountains. It was actually around 10:00 PM when we finally got into our sleeping bags to settle down for the night. As I was trying to drift off, I couldn't help but think about a conversation we'd had earlier that day with two older Swedish couples hiking together, whom we passed walking in the opposite direction. One of the ladies said it was her lifetime dream to hike the entire Kungsleden. She was very envious of the challenge we'd set ourselves, particularly as she was Swedish born and bred. Living someone else's dream, it made me feel very privileged indeed.

Day 4: Wild Camp (Vuomatjåhkka +3km) to Wild Camp (Ammarnäs +5km)

Distance:	25.1 km/15.6 miles	Elev. Gain/Loss (m):	+411/-532
Duration:	11 hours	Difficulty Level:	difficult

With clear skies above and temperatures getting below freezing during the night, we weren't surprised to find the tent covered in a thin layer of frost when we awoke the next day. It wasn't anything to complain about though, as we were far too busy relishing our first morning of complete blue skies and sunshine as far as the eye could see. Our first aim of the day was to get to the Aigert emergency shelter. It was a gentle uphill walk, so we could really take in the vast view of the valley that lay before us (or switch off and get lost in our own thoughts). It was such a surreal feeling knowing that apart from a handful of other hikers going in the opposite direction, we were really the only people for miles around.

Figure 39 – Reaching Aigert Emergency Shelter | Heading to Aigert STF Hut

Having not seen another soul for at least 16 hours, we found the Aigert emergency shelter to be a busy junction point – two groups of hikers heading southbound were just setting off as we arrived. After they had disappeared down the trail, we decided to take a quick look inside the hut and also photograph the toilet! Toileting procedures in wilderness areas usually involve going off discreetly somewhere and digging a hole. But in Sweden and what this trail definitely does well, is the provision of WC conveniences along the route! The toilets always seem to be located in the most incredibly scenic spots, too!

We reached the Aigert STF mountain hut mid-afternoon, but as it was such a nice day, we didn't venture inside. Instead, we sat on a bench, took off our boots, and enjoyed cold drinks whilst enjoying the view of the surrounding peaks. The final 8 kilometres between the hut and Ammarnäs were a steep descent, which, in all honesty, is not our hiking preference. But in this instance, the downhill momentum helped us pick up the pace and cover more ground, which we were pleased about, as we were now on a mission to reach Ammarnäs before the supermarket closed!

The trail wound its way along the mountainside towards Ammarnäs, the beautiful mountain scenery, clear skies, and striking colours certainly making this a day to remember. Then, we spied houses, meaning civilisation was close! As we walked into Ammarnäs along the main road, a guy who was busy pruning his hedge looked up and greeted us with a friendly "Welcome to Ammarnäs!". If the locals bother to speak to you, it always bodes well.

Figure 40 – Clear Skies above Beautiful Mountain Scenery| Road Walking towards Ammarnäs

Although we were aiming to reach Ammarnäs, it was not the final stop of our day. So we took our main break when we reached the village green, which is conveniently located opposite the supermarket, and hiked on a further 7 kilometres after we had refuelled with some fresh goodies from the shop. We took advice from the locals and decided on following the road out of Ammarnäs, going past the famous *Potatisbacken* (Potato Hill) and continuing uphill, following the Vindelälven (Vindel River). We picked up the pace for the last 7 kilometres of the day and pushed on, looking for a wild camp spot beside the river.

Fortunately, we came across a clearing right next to the river, complete with a picnic bench and fire pit, and a sheltered spot by some bushes a bit further up offering us some privacy from the road, perfect for pitching our tent. As soon as the sun dipped behind the fells on the other side of the river, we were plagued by bugs. They weren't mosquitoes, but more like midges. Small, flying, biting insects that are equally annoying. But the bugs were not going to put a dampener on our spirits, as it was a brilliant day to be on the trail!

Day 5: Wild Camp (Ammarnäs +5km) to Wild Camp at Sjnulttjie Shelter

Distance:	29.2 km/18.1 miles	Elev. Gain/Loss (m):	+639/-574
Duration:	11 hours	Difficulty Level:	easy

Today, we were soaking up incredible vistas and musing over the wonders of Sweden with all kinds of interesting people on our way to Adolfström. As we've found in the past, it's the human element on any long-distance hike that can really brighten your days. Whether it be between ourselves or conversing with complete strangers en route, we enjoy plenty of trail talk. We love meeting like-minded people and listening to their experiences of the world. Not only that, we become enthused by their avid descriptions of trails we've yet to set foot on. It's always good to get first-hand suggestions for future adventures! So today, we were excited to encounter several people on the trail of varying nationalities, who all stopped to talk to us!

Figure 41 – Airing Sleeping Bags on Rock | Unexpected Trail Marker

Early morning, the grassy trail made for easy walking. We covered 5 kilometres in one and a half hours, setting a really good pace for the day. The route climbed gently uphill where dense pine forest changed into a thicket of silver birch. Here, the first signs of autumn were upon us as we noticed leaves were starting to turn a beautiful, bright yellow. The sun was shining brightly, and it was even hot enough to take our coats off for a while. It felt so good that we spied a big rock and took a rest break, enjoying the rays.

On the map we used, it shows that there are two routes from Ammarnäs leading to Adolfström. The official Kungsleden route appears to go out to come back on itself, so we opted to take the more direct, alternative route to save us a few miles. This decision was also made after advice from the locals, who told us that we would still see good scenery in either direction and that most hikers now take the shorter route as the 'official' Kungsleden path anyway. The track we followed also had orange paint daubed on stones at various points, signalling the way and soon rejoined with the Kungsleden at the main trail junction.

Whilst walking along the track, we saw a helicopter transporting wooden planks and metal posts in readiness for a new *rengärde* (reindeer enclosure), built for herding and keeping the reindeer together during the winter months. It returned several times, so Wayne managed to film it flying overhead. After taking the shortcut, we were hoping to get to camp a lot earlier than previous days – well that was the plan anyway.

Figure 42 – Looking across the Entire Valley Floor | Wild Camp Spot

During the course of the day, we passed 8 hikers all heading in the opposite direction, walking southbound to Ammarnäs. It was all very interesting stopping and conversing with them about their hiking experiences on the Kungsleden so far and gleaning from them the 'what not to miss' bits, seeing as they had literally just done the sections we were about to experience for ourselves. It's always worth taking on board personal recommendations and advice, especially as we knew very little of the trail overall with the limited resources written in English out there in print and on the internet. We were genuinely surprised to have seen so many people on the trail in a single day, particularly this specific section of the trail. It has the reputation of largely being missed out due to the fact that there aren't any STF mountain hut facilities between Kvikkjokk and Ammarnäs, a 130-kilometre (81 miles) stretch of the Kungsleden where wild camping is the order of the day.

The Brits we chatted to had recommended camping by the Sjnulttjie emergency shelter, so that's where we were aiming for. It made it our longest trail day yet! We covered 29 kilometres, so that we could catch up with our planned schedule and maintain our 21-day itinerary. It also meant we would have less distance to cover the following day.

Day 6: Wild Camp at Sjnulttjie Shelter to Adolfström

Distance:	23.7 km/14.7 miles	Elev. Gain/Loss (m):	+326/-393
Duration:	11 hours	Difficulty Level:	easy

Today, the trail crossed from one administrative region to another, and we could immediately see the difference in trail maintenance. There is definitely a noticeable difference by way of large boggy areas and not so many wooden boards. We also found there to be lots of broken boards and heavy erosion of the trail, as foot traffic had widened the trail with people trying to avoid the worst sections of ground. As we were constantly watching our footing and trying to avoid the worst of it ourselves, it slowed down our pace somewhat.

Figure 43 – Suspension Bridge over Fast Flowing River | Tea Break at Badasjåkkå Hut

Wayne was struggling with his feet and took some painkillers to take his mind off his blisters. Due to this and the fact we needed to tackle some laundry and take a shower, we had decided that we would stay in the church hostel in Jäkkvik the next evening. With it being recommended by every hiker we passed that had already stopped there, we would be foolish not to make the most of the opportunity.

But before that, we reached another little gem right on the Kungsleden by way of the little settlement of Bäverholmen. Just as the Brits had said, there is a fantastic restaurant/café named *Värdshus*, selling homemade cakes and pastries, freshly baked onsite by a lovely lady chef who speaks good English. We had been in pursuit of cake all day, and it is the perfect place for a pit-stop before continuing on to Adolfström. There is even camping on the green next to the restaurant with use of showers and utility block if you feel like hanging your boots up for the day.

Figure 44 – Walking through Dense Woodland | Cake Break at Värdshus Café

We walked the last 8 kilometres into Adolfström around the Iraft lake, which was a woodland walk with rocks and roots to navigate, but we were just on a mission to get to town! Reaching Adolfström around 7:30 PM, we were much too late for resupplying at the shop. This late in August, it had limited daily opening times. As the shop wasn't going to be open until 9:00 AM the following morning, we had to rethink our plans about the following day, especially as signage from Adolfström said Jäkkvik was 27 kilometres away, not the 21 kilometres we had worked out from the map.

Along the main road in Adolfström, there is a helicopter tour business with camping and rental cabins at the rear, which is where we chose to stay. Further down the road, there are also other caravan and campsites on either side of the street.

Day 7: Adolfström to Jäkkvik

Distance:	21.7 km/13.5 miles	Elev. Gain/Loss (m):	+589/-604
Duration:	9 hours	Difficulty Level:	moderate

As we had hardly any food supplies left, it was our earliest start yet. We had broken camp and were back on the trail by 7:00 AM. We wanted to break the day into three 7-kilometre sections, thinking that our own map calculations were correct and that the signage saying Jäkkvik was a distance of 27 kilometres must be wrong. Initially, we found ourselves wandering through woodland, traversing slippery rocks and roots that was hard-going on our ankles. It was also uphill at first. What made matters worse was that it started raining about half an hour into our walk. We put on our waterproof gear and just braved it, keeping our heads down and pushing on. Luckily, to keep us going, we had 12 squares of chocolate left, so we ate that with gusto!

The woodland thinned out and lead us to a rocky walk around a lake, where Wayne actually slipped and fell over. Thankfully, he didn't do any permanent damage to himself or his gear! Our boots had already reached saturation point by then because of navigating so much bog. Again, there were not too many boards used on this section to assist you across and keep you dry. Our backpack straps were wet, but our waterproof jackets and trousers were holding up well and we felt warm. Our plan was to keep going until we reached the first hut marked on our map with a square symbol. We didn't know if this would be a private cabin as the other emergency huts/shelters are marked with a triangle.

Figure 45 – Reaching Pieljekaisestugan Hut | Cosy and Well-Maintained Interior

The hut named *Pieljekaisestugan* was simply an AMAZING place! With two picnic benches, a gas stove, cooking utensils, and large wood burner, it was everything we could have wanted right at that moment. It was cosy and seemed very new and well-maintained, but there were books with visitor notes dating back as far as 1983. Some kind trail angel had also left a few packets of freeze-dried vegetables on the table with a note saying take what you want.

After leaving the hut, we headed uphill beyond the treeline onto open moorland on top of the fell. By this point, the rain was really lashing down, and we were completely exposed up there. Across the top, we met Barbara heading in the opposite direction, and even though we were all soaked, we still stopped to chat. She was finishing the Kungsleden but had been hiking in Norway and hitchhiked across to do the southern section. She was the first person we had come across that suggested we skip the northern section of the trail, claiming it is so busy and touristy. After that brief encounter, we quickened our pace and soon made it to the next hut – a bigger version of the one we had utilised earlier with similar facilities. (Unnamed on the map.) Two Swedes, on a fishing trip, had already made themselves comfortable inside the hut and were waiting out the rain, as it was now coming down heavily again.

Figure 46 – Hostel in Jäkkvik | Wonderful Kitchen Facilities

With 3 kilometres or so to go to reach Jäkkvik, it was downhill from the hut. We arrived in town around 4:30 PM, our earliest finish time so far. The church hostel that was recommended to us, *Kyrkans Fjällgård*, was straight across the main road next to the lake. At a cost of 280 SEK (£24) per person for a bed, it is cheaper than an STF hut and an excellent place to stay to have a hot shower and catch up on some laundry and Wi-Fi. The hostel is very relaxed and has a large kitchen, dining area, and lounge with comfy seats, where hikers hang out and share their adventures. Upstairs, there are several large rooms with bunks that are dormitory style, but, luckily, we found a private 2-person room that was perfect for us.

We off-loaded our gear in there and then headed to the shop – a general convenience store joined to petrol station just up the main road. It is well-stocked with everything you could possibly need to resupply with on the trail, so we splurged and got four days' worth of supplies and some goodies for dinner. As we had proper facilities, Wayne cooked up a cheese burger feast for dinner, which other hikers staying in the hostel seemed very envious of! After today's efforts, it was a great reward. We were also relieved that our estimated mileage had been correct. It was, in fact, a little over 21km to Jäkkvik from Adolfström – thank goodness!

Day 8: Jäkkvik to Wild Camp (Vuonatjviken +2.5km)

Distance:	26.8 km/16.7 miles	Elev. Gain/Loss (m):	+363/-318
Duration:	10.5 hours	Difficulty Level:	easy

Making the most of the hostel facilities, we didn't leave Jäkkvik until 10:00 AM, which was a late hiking start considering we had two boat crossings today. However, it was only 17 kilometres to reach the paid-for boat crossing over Lake Riebnes to Vuonatjviken, so we knew it wasn't going to be such a long day.

As we left the hostel, we tried to ring the telephone number given on the noticeboard to find out boat crossing times, but there was no answer. We thought we might be lucky with catching a boat ride back across the lake if southbounders travelled over on the 5 o'clock boat that evening. The general consensus when talking to other hikers was that there was a morning boat crossing around 9:00 AM and an early evening crossing around 5:00 PM. With leaving Jäkkvik quite late, we didn't know if we'd get there for 5:00 PM, but as we had generally been hiking 3 kilometres in an hour, we agreed with minimal rest breaks we should push on and go for it.

It was damp and dreary when we first hit the trail. After about 4 kilometres, we got to Tjårvekallegiehtje lake, which was to be our first rowing boat crossing on the trail. By then, the sun was just about breaking through. There were two boats our side thankfully so that saved us (or rather it saved Wayne) rowing across three times, as there's always got to be one boat left on each side. We had a quick drink in the shelter and decided to bite the bullet and get going. Both boats had a lot of rain water in the bottom of the hull, so we had a brain wave and used a carrier bag to collect and empty out the water, so as to keep our packs as dry as possible. Wayne managed fine with the oars and did a great job of rowing. My task was simply to do some filming of it! On reaching the other side of the lake, you have to clip the boat on a hook and use a ratchet to pull the boat up out of the water. That was a hard job – I wouldn't have been able to do it without Wayne. The boat safely attached, it was a successful first boat crossing! We were glad that for our first try it was all of 500 metres!

Figure 47 – Shelter Next to Lake | Rowing across Tjårvekallegiehtje Lake

We were on track to reach the second boat crossing if we kept going. It was 3 kilometres uphill, 3 kilometres flattish walking across the top of the fell, then a 1-kilometre descent to reach the lake. We had already been warned it would be very muddy and slippery going both up and down, and the fact that it was raining again compounded the situation. Effectively, we were walking up a flowing stream with all the run-out. The ground was saturated so much, in the end we just had to trudge straight through the boggy sections as there was just no way around. The ground was that waterlogged and the trail so poorly maintained. Our boots had reached saturation point hours ago, so we had wet, soggy socks and feet all day. Wayne had slipped over for a second time, but thankfully again it was nothing serious.

We arrived at the lakeside at exactly 5:00 PM. We predicted that if the boat left the other side at 5:00 PM (as other hikers had told us), it would reach our side by around 5:30 PM. That time came and went but there was still no sign of a boat. Deciding that we'd give it until 6:00 PM, we moved into the porch of one of the private huts a bit further up the bank, as it was sheltered and there was a stool to sit on. I tried the phone number again that we'd got from the hostel earlier that morning. This time someone answered. It was the skipper's wife and thankfully she spoke some English. She explained that her husband was bringing four people across the lake at 6:30 PM and would take us back with him. On hearing that news, we were extremely grateful!

The journey across Lake Riebnes was short, 20 minutes maximum, but the lake was long. There's no way you'd be able to row across this one. The journey across to Vuonatjviken village was about 6 kilometres, but it seemed to go on forever! This was the most expensive boat journey at 300 SEK (£26) per person, as it is privately run, unlike most of the other crossing that are operated by the STF and typically cost 200 SEK (£17). I had my photo taken with the skipper after he'd moored up and tied off, but then it was my turn to slip and fall over on a large rock, as we headed away from the shore.

Figure 48 – Seeking Shelter while Waiting | Pic with Skipper after Crossing Lake Riebnes

As cabins at the Vuonatjviken holiday village are more than 1000 SEK per night, we decided against a cosy warm cabin for the night, instead opting to hike a further 2 kilometres on more wet, slippery mud and rock to reach the Bartek river, where we thought there'd be some good camping spots. As the skipper confirmed, camping is free!

Day 9: Wild Camp (Vuonatjviken +2.5km) to Wild Camp (Tjaurakatan)

Distance:	18.9 km/11.7 miles	Elev. Gain/Loss (m):	+130/-101
Duration:	8.5 hours	Difficulty Level:	easy

Day 9 seemed particularly promising with lovely blue skies and the sun overhead. Although, when we set off again after breakfast, the ground was still sodden from the previous couple of days' rain. It was tiresome having to pay due care and attention to where we placed our feet, but having already slipped over, both of us luckily getting away with just scrapes and bruises, we knew every step we took could be potentially hazardous.

We found the first 6 kilometres quite tough going with the weight of our packs, after pushing ourselves yesterday to reach the boat crossing in time, which was compounded even more by having to go uphill, stepping on roots and rocks. Yet, this tiresome section of trail was instantly made better by passing several lakes with lovely cloud reflections, where we stopped to take photographs and enjoy the view.

It seemed like forever to hike up and out of the treeline today. When we finally got onto the open plateau, we were treated to extensive views of the surrounding mountains and lakes and could see autumnal colours of red and orange coming through in the heather. There were some reindeer grazing on the plain, which we tried to film, but they were very skittish and kept running away. The ground was still boggy in places but much better than earlier, so we managed to stride out and cover a good distance at a faster pace. We came across two hikers completing the 'Green Ribbon Trail'. They had already been hiking for around 20 days and had given themselves 6 weeks to complete the trek from the point where Sweden, Norway, and Finland meet in the north to Grövelsjön in the southern Swedish mountains.

Figure 49 – Incredible Lake Reflections Panorama

The high point of today was well over 1000 metres, taller than any mountain in England! From this spot, we could see one massive expanse of moorland rolling out ahead to a series of lakes with some giant peaks in the distance. It was amazing to think we were here in all of this with no one else for many kilometres around. We soon spotted the emergency shelter – this one truly rustic in the ancient Lappish style, with a little wooden door and a roof made out of mud and moss. Inside, there was just a fire pit in the middle, but the shelter would be a godsend in heavy rain or cold.

As we neared the stream, but before we got to the bridge, we spotted a great pre-used campsite – complete with fire pit and wooden planks on stones already set up as seats. We still really had over a kilometre to go to reach where we had planned on camping, but as this spot looked so nice and still had the sun on it, we decided to set up camp early. We erected the tent, then both went on a mission to find some wood for the fire. Whilst gathering fallen twigs, I noticed that the blueberries were looking much bigger so must be ripening ready for harvest. I couldn't wait to pick some more and have them with muesli for breakfast. It was a lovely sunset, one of the first we had really seen, where the sky had a pink glow all around. But it got cold quickly, so we soon escaped to the tent to get warm and prepare ourselves for a 30-kilometre mammoth day tomorrow.

Day 10: Wild Camp (Tjaurakatan) to Wild Camp (Suonergarssa)

Distance:	25.8 km /16 miles	Elev. Gain/Loss (m):	+127/-231
Duration:	10 hours	Difficulty Level:	easy

We set the alarm for 5:45 AM to be away around 7:00 AM, as we'd planned on a 30-kilometre day. After getting going and witnessing a cloud inversion from above the valley, the Kungsleden headed downhill towards Tjieggelvas lake. The next 16 kilometres or so were through boggy, waterlogged meadows on low ground, which were bug infested hell zones. Our feet were soaked again as there were just not enough wooden boards laid in the worst areas – if any. We also had to resort to wearing our head nets at one point as there were swarms of midges hovering around us and clouds of mosquitoes on the attack. We couldn't decide if we smelt good or really quite bad to be attracting them in such large numbers! Just from this brief encounter with the pests, we can definitely see the benefits of hiking later in the season. They were too annoying to stop and rest properly, so we pushed on, aiming for the treeline, where it would be cooler and hopefully bug-free. Of all the days we wanted a breeze to keep them at bay, but one wasn't forthcoming.

Figure 50 – Early Morning on the Trail | First Time Wearing Head Nets

We met an older couple hiking in wellies, who told us that we'd be ankle deep in bog water at the bottom of the valley and there'd be no avoiding it! We had previously read about Swedes hiking the Kungsleden in wellies and weren't sure how true this was – but having seen this couple, it was obviously their preferred choice of footwear – not a very comfortable option in our opinion, however, if you're going the full 430 kilometres. But with news of the bog, they also brought with them much better news about the weather. The forecast had changed from when we last looked. So instead of rain today and tomorrow, we could now expect clouds today and sunshine tomorrow, a much better prognosis.

Figure 51 – Heading into the Mountains | Wild Campsite Overlooking U-Shaped Valley

As we traversed rocks and roots and faced more slippery sections of trail, it became a bit of a trudge once more with us cursing the lower woodland sections. Here, the vegetation was noticeably different. Instead of walking through a canopy of silver birch trees, we were moving through a denser pine forest, which smells wonderful and literally gives you a spring in your step, as the trail is littered with thousands of pine needles, which makes for a good spongy landing.

Our mission was now to get above treeline again by 2:00 PM, having decided that we wouldn't head for the mountain hut as that meant heading back down to lower ground and more dreaded bog. We thought that we'd look for a camp spot along the river whilst heading down off the ridge but still above the treeline, where there would hopefully be a breeze. We found an ideal flattish spot next to some fallen boulders that was out of the wind and mosquito-free – perfect as neither of us could walk much more. We had both made use of painkillers today to keep us moving relatively pain-free. We went to sleep that evening very excited at the thought that we'd be officially crossing into the Arctic Circle the next day.

Day 11: Wild Camp (Suonergarssa) to Kvikkjokk

Distance:	22.1 km/13.7 miles	Elev. Gain/Loss (m):	+248/-388
Duration:	6.5 hours	Difficulty Level:	easy

We estimated that we had about 16 kilometres to walk today to get to the boat crossing that would take us to Kvikkjokk, roughly the halfway point on the Kungsleden. So we decided on an early start to try and benefit from the comforts of the mountain station for as long as possible. Yes, we intended on overnighting there! We were firing on all cylinders as there were blue skies ahead, and it looked to be an amazing day weather-wise! Wayne even got the drone out and flew it over the campsite before we set off.

We found ourselves weaving through birch trees, then pine forest once again. The pine needles provided the trail with perfect ground cover, which was spongy and light, and the smell of which was just heaven. We startled some reindeer grazing right next to the trail, as we powered on with our heads down, which in fact startled us, too! We didn't hear or see them until we were within a foot away, the wind blowing through our ears and our minds wandering away. And neither did they hear us. Yet, we were still too late to get a close-up photo, as they scattered immediately and bounded off. Frustrated by our inability to capture them on camera, we were also disappointed that having passed into the Arctic Circle, denoted by a line on the map, there was no signage on the trail signifying this.

Figure 52 – Quick Rest Break at Tsielekjåhkå Shelter | Bridge over Tsielekjåhkå River

It was an easy rock hop to cross the river, followed by a steep descent to reach the lakeside. The flatter sections along the valley bottom had wooden boards in the wetter sections, which we were grateful of now that our feet and boots were finally dry. We could see the hut from afar, which spurred us on all the more. Arriving just after 1:00 PM, we didn't know it, but we were extremely lucky to have arrived at that time, as Helena, the boat crossing lady, was already waiting at the hut to take someone across Lake Saggat. She told us that a storm had knocked out the power at Kvikkjokk, so the phone lines were down, making it impossible to phone for the boat. She was leaving a note to say that she would come back across the lake and collect anyone waiting at 5:00 PM. Thankfully, we arrived before she left and crossed straight away.

Figure 53 – Taking the Boat Across Lake Saggat | Private Room at Kvikkjokk Fjällstation

After a scenic boat crossing, Helena showed us the way to the Kvikkjokk mountain station, and we arrived around 2:00 PM. Thankfully, the power was back on, otherwise we'd have had to change our plans, and we were really desperate to do some laundry. The only shop in Kvikkjokk is at the mountain station. Everything is around double what you'd pay in a normal supermarket, but there is more choice than at a mountain hut.

The worst bit about today was that Wayne somehow managed to snap his hiking pole. Ingenious as ever, he managed to fix it though with a good idea and bit of perseverance. I love hiking with a proper Bear Grylls!

Day 12: Kvikkjokk to Wild Camp (Pårte +4km)

Distance:	19.7 km/12.2 miles	Elev. Gain/Loss (m):	+293/-249
Duration:	8.5 hours	Difficulty Level:	easy

Today, we were over halfway on our Kungsleden journey and beginning the northern section. It proved to be a fairly easy day, as we were hiking just 19 kilometres to our planned wild camp spot, having decided on breaking the next three days into four to allow for us to make a detour off the Kungsleden to the Skierfe lookout point. It was all uphill out of Kvikkjokk, but after a couple of days of better weather, the ground was finally drying and the muddy sections were a lot easier to navigate. Wayne classifies three types of mud on this trail – bog mud, bad mud, and good mud – each very distinctive in how far you sink in and what annoyance it does to your boots! We had a couple of water breaks and rested our feet, not really because we were tired but more for the fact that there were wooden planks on stones serving as makeshift benches right next to streams we had to cross. It's unbelievable how much you miss a proper seat when you have to sit on the floor or on a rock!

Figure 54 – Full Pack after Resupplying in Kvikkjokk | Familiar Boardwalks

We hiked 16 kilometres and got to the Pårte hut at 2:30 PM. Day use at the huts is typically between 11:00 AM and 3:00 PM, so we made it in time to use the gas and sit inside at a table with chairs! The warden at the hut was very welcoming and added a few extra touches, such as providing a jug of lemonade on the front porch with a sign saying "Rest your feet and help yourself!". We set off around 4:00 PM, intending on hiking just 3 kilometres farther before finding a camp spot. We've learnt now that wherever the trail crosses a larger stream or river, it is almost certain that there will be an established campsite (often with a makeshift fire pit). Along the way, the trail was getting busier with hikers all aiming to get to Pårte – and as usual, we were the only two hiking in the direction of north! It was a bit wet and muddy by the first bridge we came to, so we pushed on to the second bridge and found several camp spots located on both sides of the trail. We picked the flattest, pitched the tent, and started gathering fallen wood to get the fire going.

Day 13: Wild Camp (Pårte +4km) to Skierfe Detour (1km off-trail)

Distance:	23.8 km/14.8 miles	Elev. Gain/Loss (m):	+379/-372
Duration:	12.5 hours	Difficulty Level:	difficult

It rained through the night and continued when we got up, which had not been the forecast. There was low cloud in the valley and a virtual white-out when we ventured out of tent. But we just had to get on with things, pack the tent away wet and hope for better weather later to dry it out. We decided on getting going and having breakfast 5 kilometres along the way at the Jagge shelter. It was an uphill climb through mountain forest, which was very muddy, so our waterproof trousers and boots did their job but were wet again before long. We made it to the hut within a couple of hours, where a Swedish couple, hiking five days from Saltoluokta to Kvikkjokk was already staying. They quickly made room for us and invited us in, then proceeded to off-load some of their surplus goods onto us, which we were grateful to receive. We decided to stay put a while longer and wait out the rain, which was now coming down heavily once more. It was a good decision, as it dried up quickly following the final downpour.

Figure 55 – Early Morning White Out | Looking onto the Bårddegiehtje Mountains

As the clouds cleared, they revealed huge mountains with a river delta below. It looked stunning, as we had been waiting for scenery like this for a while. We found a rock to sit on and admire the view whilst eight people hiked up the valley in little waves. We set off again downhill, heading for the lakeside, where we would take another boat crossing over to Aktse. There is the option of rowing, but seeing as Wayne would get the short straw and end up doing that job (again), he said he would rather pay the 200 SEK (£17) per person, more for peace of mind that we'd actually make it all the way across safely. The only downside of taking the boat is that it is fixed times.

On our side of the lake it was 9:15 AM and 5:15 PM. As we arrived around 3:00 PM, we had a couple of hours waiting in the hut before the jetty. From the southern side of the lake, you have to put up a white flag to signal you want to cross in case there is no one wanting to travel south from the Aktse side.

From the jetty, it's a 1-kilometre walk to the STF hut at Aktse along wooden planks most of the way. One of the STF cabins was having renovation work done so that it will have a large supply shop for the next hiking season. Currently, goods are housed in a lockable tin shed, where you help yourself to what you want and put money in a tin (rather like an extra-large honesty box). There was a good selection of food stuffs and even some hiking gear for sale, such as a scarf, head torch, postcards, and beer in a bucket of ice. The hut also has an outdoor shower. It is cold water piped downhill from a natural spring, but there is the luxury of a proper shower head! We just reccied the facilities, then decided that we'd continue up the ridge to the top of the valley to the Skierfe/Kungsleden junction.

Figure 56 – Arriving on the North Shore of Lake Laitaure| Boardwalks Leading to Akste

A German guys told us that we could camp at the junction, then leave our stuff and effectively day-hike to the Skierfe lookout point over the Rapa delta. This way, we didn't have to go up there with heavy, cumbersome packs. We asked the warden at the hut about availability of camping and water, and he said there was currently both. He recommended continuing on the Skierfe trail for around half hour where there'd be a large rock with good camping nearby. It looked like it was going to be a good sunset, so off we went up the ridge line and onto the Skierfe trail, reaching the point he recommended about 7:30 PM. It was not such an easy task finding water, but there was a spring a little further uphill from our campsite, where we could fill up our bottles and make sure we had enough for the rest of the hike in the morning.

Day 14: Skierfe Detour (1km from Kungsleden trail) to Wild Camp (Sitojaure +5km)

Distance:	28.2 km/17.5 miles	Elev. Gain/Loss (m):	+431/-447
Duration:	10.5 hours	Difficulty Level:	moderate

We awoke abruptly to grunting and the jangling of bells. It was reindeer foraging around our tent! It was a little after 7:00 AM, and the sun was already warming our tent, which we were grateful of after it being so wet the day before. That meant it should completely dry out, and our down bags would fluff up nicely after a bit of heat. We enjoyed a leisurely breakfast, taking in the view of the Rapadalen from our camp spot. We had fantastic blue skies with great lighting, which would be perfect for photography from the top of Skierfe. What a difference a day makes!

Setting off up the trail around 9:15 AM with our backpacks only filled with water, snacks, and camera gear, we didn't think it would take us more than an hour to reach the lookout point on top of the flat summit. Our packs felt empty in comparison to what we usually carry, having left the tent behind with virtually everything else. However, we had underestimated how long it would take by an hour, it actually being 6 kilometres from where we camped and two hours to reach the summit. But there were only two other people on top of Skierfe when we arrived, who, after chatting with us, were keen to see the drone in action and what footage we could get of the delta. (Since our hike, drone laws have changed in Sweden, and it is no longer legal to fly them!)

Figure 57 – Selfie on top of Skierfe | Aerial Shot from the Summit

From the big flat rock on top of the summit, you have the best lookout position and our view today in such good weather was incredible! The sun was glinting off one of the tributaries, reflecting a delicate ball of brightness.

Looking down from above, each channel looked like a ribbon weaving its way across the valley floor, each a striking colour ranging from dark strands of inky blue black to icy emerald green caused by silt in the glacial waters. It felt like you were witnessing the earth from a position in space, like the photographs you see from NASA. We stayed up there for about an hour, before the temperature began to drop and the weather started to change. Our first mission of the day was done, but we still had to get back to camp, pack the tent and gear away, and reach the lake on the other side of the plateau to take us across to Sitojaure.

We got back to camp around 1:30 PM, had a quick lunch, broke camp, then set off back to the trail junction to get back on the Kungsleden. We had around 8 kilometres to go to reach the lake. First uphill to get over the ridge, the high point being 940 metres, then a flattish section to cover taking us across the plateau, then a steep downhill to the lakeside. There was lots more autumnal colour as the scrubby ground cover was changing to a deep red.

Figure 58 – Delta of the Rapa River | Wilds of Sarek National Park

There is a sign at the top of the plateau explaining that you need to call to arrange boat transportation from this point, as it is the only area with a cell phone signal. We phoned several times but there was no answer, so we left a message that we'd arrive at the lakeside hopefully in time to get the boat around 5:30 PM. Luckily, we made it over the plateau and down to the lake for just after 5:00 PM, where there were already seven people waiting on the jetty. We hoped there'd be enough room for us.

The warden from the Sitojaure hut was also getting a ride back across the lake after hiking up Skierfe that morning. She asked if we were intending on staying at the hut or pushing on further to camp up the trail. As our map again showed no water, we weren't quite sure. She suggested there was water and camp spots around 3 kilometres up the trail, so we decided that we'd continue to give us less miles the following day as we were heading for the Fjällstation at Saltoluokta. In actual fact, we pushed on about another 5 kilometres as we looked for running water and a sufficient camp spot. Two other couples were also hiking our way now – something we're not used to at all, especially having to overtake!

Figure 59 – Heading down to Lake Sitojaure | Cooking Dinner whilst Watching Sunset

We found water, but as the grassy camp spots were lower and near boggy areas and there were a lot of bugs around, we decided to camp higher, but at the expense of it being on rougher, scrubbier ground. As we didn't want to puncture our sleep pads with any twigs or scrubby bits poking through the base of our tent, and as we didn't have a separate ground sheet, we laid out our maps, made from waterproof durable material, and positioned the tent on top for extra protection. By the time we were ready for bed, we witnessed beautiful sunset colours at the end of the valley over a small lake, the sky such a deep pink then red. It literally looked as though it were on fire. All in all, it was a very successful hiking and photography day!

Day 15: Wild Camp (Sitojaure +5km) to Saltoluokta

Distance:	14.8 km/9.2 miles	Elev. Gain/Loss (m):	+146/-262
Duration:	6 hours	Difficulty Level:	easy

What a day! After such a wonderful evening, the morning brought with it the most dreadful weather since we had started hiking the Kungsleden. We awoke at 6:00 AM to driving rain and strong winds battering the tent, so we quickly packed everything away and decided to get going and power it to the emergency hut – 6 kilometres further along the trail. With a cold, biting wind lashing our faces and heavy rain pouring down continuously, we were quickly drenched through.

The trail continued across the top of the plateau for what seemed like an endless amount of time, with no letting up from the wind or rain, not even for a brief interlude. The trail was away with run-off as the ground had become so saturated, it felt like we were wading up a stream for quite some way. All we could focus on was getting to the hut in the quickest time possible – with our hoods up and heads down. Just when I was feeling really miserable about the whole experience and wishing I was anywhere but here, we smelt smoke in the air and knew the hut must be close. Even more welcoming was the fact that someone was in it already and they'd lit a fire! Then, as if by magic, the hut revealed itself through the white-out in the distance and we instantly quickened our pace some more.

Figure 60 – Braving the Turbulent Weather | Cabin at Saltoluokta Fjällstation

We reached the hut, sopping wet through, where a Swedish guy and Dutch lady were inside drying out. The guy had actually spent the night in the hut with a bad ankle after hiking for five days in Sarek National Park. Despite his ailments, he was extremely chatty, as he said he'd not spoken to anyone else in all that time. The lady was cycling part of the Kungsleden so had a mountain bike with her. We de-layered, grateful of the wood burning stove, and hung our wet gear up to dry, then warmed ourselves through with hot chocolates and hot muesli. We arrived at the hut around 9:30 AM and stayed for around an hour as our gear was almost dry and nicely warmed up ready for round two. By now, other people were also arriving for their own little bit of respite.

We set off again, hoping the bad weather had abated somewhat, but no such luck. We saw a sign that Saltoluokta was only 3 kilometres away which gave us extra energy. The trail was a mixture of rocks, sand, mud, and gushing water, so we still had to watch our footing, but we seemed to make it to Saltoluokta in no time. As we hurried down to the huts, we predicted it would be similar to Kvikkjokk mountain station – but overall, we were quite

< 6. Personal Experience >

disappointed with the standard of facilities provided at premium prices. We wanted a private room, but even with STF discount it was 1,300 SEK (£112), so instead we opted for a shared 4-bed dorm, just on principle.

Figure 61 – 4-Person Dorm Room | Resupplying from the Saltoluokta Store

The shop at Saltoluokta has the usual goods expected for hiking as well as gear items. We chose carefully as it is easy to spend 500 SEK (£43) on only a few items! For dinner that night, the best value meal was a 500-gram bag of pasta, a jar of green pesto, and a tin of tuna. We made use of the Wi-Fi in the reception area before heading back to our room at 10:00 PM. We were grateful that it wouldn't be a rush in the morning, as we had both a boat and bus connection to get us to the other side of the valley before the Kungsleden continued.

Day 16: Saltoluokta to Teusajaure STF Hut

Distance:	45 km/28 miles*	Elev. Gain/Loss (m):	+174/-153
Duration:	7.5 hours	Difficulty Level:	moderate

*(includes 30 km/18.6 miles by bus)

We had quite an unsettled sleep due to snoring from other guests in the room. This is another such reason that we prefer a private room and to camp. We awoke early anyway in readiness for our breakfast feast! The restaurant was already a hive of activity. Everyone was busy slicing bread and making sandwiches like they'd not eaten for a week.

Boat and bus times restricted us to a late hiking start. The boat was really busy, the bus not so much. Hikers continuing on the Kungsleden generally got on the bus, whereas the weekenders picked up their cars after disembarking the boat. The bus journey to Vakkotavare is only around 30 kilometres, but it took us almost two hours, as 55 minutes are spent at a tourist shop/restaurant after about ten minutes into your journey, where you have to change buses, then continue with a new driver.

The bus dropped us off outside the Vakkotavare STF hut just before 2:30 PM. We didn't check out the hut as we were intent on hiking up out of the valley straight away. As soon as we got on the top and it levelled out over a plateau, we could feel the difference in temperature. There were lots of bulbous, ripe blueberries ready for the picking but we didn't linger too long as there was a biting wind and cold chill running through our veins. It was the first time we'd actually hiked with full hat, gloves, and warm mid-layer under our waterproof jackets. Ominous looking clouds above pelted down some hail stones but were gone after a few minutes. Then, it was back to blue skies, intermittent sunshine, and a crisp chill in the air, keeping our cheeks and lips chapped cold but giving us a rosy glow.

Figure 62 – All-You-Can-Eat Breakfast | Taking the Boat from Saltoluokta to Kebnats

We stopped for a break after about 6 kilometres, the wind dying down enough for us to sit for a while, have a snack, and enjoy the view. It was a really stunning valley with peaks on both sides, many covered in snow on the summits. As it was so cold, we decided to camp this side of the lake to be near the emergency hut, should we need to cook and get warm in it. That also meant leaving the boat crossing until morning when Wayne would be much fresher for rowing! As it turned out, three Brits were just disembarking from one rowing boat as we got to the lake. There was another boat already tethered there and a third boat was just making its way into shore. The final couple to arrive would have had to row three times to leave a boat on the other side if we were not going to cross. It felt mean saying we were staying this side, so the people were very grateful that we said we would continue and row over tonight. Thankfully, Wayne agreed even though I'd technically volunteered him for the task!

As the light was so good, and it looked a nice hut right next to the jetty, we decided that we'd camp at the Teusajaure mountain hut and make the most of the location and facilities, which included a sauna. That was an experience in itself! As it was already 7:30 PM, we left our packs where we wanted to pitch the tent and headed straight for the sauna. Seeing several naked guys run out into the lake, plus a naked woman washing outside, we decided to be brave and do it the Swedish way and go in naked ourselves!

Figure 63 – Stony Trail Leads down to Lake Teusajaure | Rowing across the Lake

After freshening up, we pitched the tent, then went inside the hut to cook dinner. It was almost dark in there, so people had candles burning at their tables. In 16 days, there has been so much change – the nights are drawing in and the evenings are much cooler. It is a very short summer season in Sweden anyway, but it definitely feels like winter is on its way!

Day 17: Teusajaure STF Hut to Wild Camp (-1km from Singi STF Hut)

Distance:	21.1 km/13.1 miles	Elev. Gain/Loss (m):	+105/-86
Duration:	8 hours	Difficulty Level:	easy

What an amazing camp spot! We awoke to beautiful lake reflections, and it was a lovely morning. After packing our gear away for what felt like the 100th time, we headed on up the trail, leaving around 9:30 AM. It was a steep ascent up the side of the waterfall, leaving Teusajaure behind at the foot of the lake. It took it out of us first thing as we were severely lacking in calories compared to yesterday's quadruple breakfast feast at Saltoluokta. We had only 9 kilometres to go to reach the next hut at Kaitumjaure, but it seemed a long 9 kilometres. What we had assumed would be a gentle walk along the river was another ankle buster over a trail littered with rocks and boulders that meant concentration was paramount every step of the way. It soon becomes wearing on both your feet and your mood.

It was a welcome relief when we arrived at the Kaitumjaure hut around 1:15 PM. We were impressed with the large shop, new toilet block, and new sauna, which we were sad not to get to sample as this was just a quick rest and recharge lunch stop using the hut's day facilities for free – courtesy of having Hostelling International cards. The shop was well-stocked and had a better selection of goodies than Saltoluokta. The warden pointed out a moose and its young calf grazing across the river. It's the first one we've seen, albeit from a distance, but even from so far away it still looked huge!

Figure 64 – Reflections on Lake Teusajaure | Suspension Bridge over Tjäktjajåkka River

We had around an hour's rest, then set back off up the trail. The valley rolled out before us, gradually taking us north where we could see bigger mountains in the distance. The warden had told us it had been snowing beyond Singi this morning, so we hoped it was only a flurry and wouldn't continue when we hiked that section the next day. The trail was a lot better along the valley, much less stony. Three kilometres before Singi, we started looking for a good place to camp. We found a spot down in a sheltered dip, just off the main trail right by a stream. It was grassy and dry, with a slight breeze funnelling through, all the prerequisites we like. We hoped it wouldn't be too cold a night, but the next few nights will certainly test our gear, as we'll be sleeping at over 800 metres.

Day 18: Wild Camp (-1km from Singi STF Hut) to Wild Camp (Tjäktja STF Hut +1km)

Distance:	26.4 km/16.4 miles	Elev. Gain/Loss (m):	+474/-391
Duration:	12 hours	Difficulty Level:	difficult

As we woke up, we were pleasantly surprised that it wasn't raining and the tent was dry. It was only a kilometre or so to the Singi STF hut, so no sooner had we got going, than we stopped again to dispose of our rubbish in the recycling bins and use the toilets. We chatted with the hosts who were impressed with our fast pace and the fact we were hiking the entire Kungsleden in the unusual way of south to north. I had a photo with them stood on the porch, whilst Wayne was quizzed about which was his favourite football team in the premiership.

We set off again, the skies above us cloudy but bright, looking a bit more ominous down the valley in the direction we were heading. It was around 6 kilometres to the next emergency shelter, where we had planned on having a tea break. It was busy around the hut with people sitting outside and coming and going. But it was there that the rain clouds came in, so we quickly got our waterproof gear ready and went inside the hut to finish our drinks. The hut was laid out the same way as the previous emergency shelters we had visited. What was disappointing, however, was a giant pile of rubbish left in the entrance porch. In this very busy section between Abisko and Nikkaluokta, where people take a detour to hike up Kebnekaise, it was already evident that people do not follow the hiker rule of pack it in, pack it out, which is very frustrating for hikers in the true sense as opposed to day trippers!

Figure 65 – Another Scenic Toilet Location | Chatting with the Wardens at STF Singi

We set off down the valley again, heading next for the Sälka STF hut, where we were going to make use of the day facilities and have some lunch. The wind and rain was intermittent along the way, sometimes heavy, but not quite soaking us through. It was much more bearable than the day we were heading for Saltoluokta! We reached the hut around 2:00 PM. The shop area was very busy, not so the day use hut, which we were surprised about. There was only one other couple using it, long-distance hikers like ourselves, tackling the Kungsleden south to north. They had changed plans on which direction after arriving and finding out that the Fjällräven event was in full flow with 2,000 people on the northern section of the trail. Not wanting to hike amongst that many people, they hitch-hiked to Hemavan and started there instead. We would have done the same thing!

We got going again around 3:00 PM for the final push. We wanted to reach the end of the valley and hike up and over Tjäktja Pass, the highest point on the entire Kungsleden trail at 1,140 metres. It was 8 kilometres to the emergency hut at the top of the pass and, although it was only a steady 200-metre climb, after 3 hours of solid walking, we felt drained and needed a quick burst of energy. So we took off our packs and had five minutes admiring the valley view, looking back to where we'd spent the last several hours walking and shared a bag of jelly sweets. After the false summit, you steadily wind up another steep section of the pass behind, when all of a sudden the mountain hut comes into view!

We arrived around 6:30 PM and used the hut to make dinner as it was both warm and dry. It was a further 3 kilometres to the next mountain hut, so we decided that we'd camp before or after it wherever there was a stream close by for a water supply. We'd already been warned by a hiker coming in the opposite direction that after the pass, it was 4 kilometres over a rocky boulder field that was hard-going on the feet. We were pleasantly surprised to find that it wasn't as bad as we were expecting. Having our bellies full with hot food, we were moving at a good pace, quickly reaching the next STF hut, Tjäktja, around 8:30 PM. To access the hut, you have to leave the Kungsleden and cross the river. As we didn't want to pay the camp fee, we continued on the proper trail, finding a camp spot with access down to the river on the other side, still in view of the hut but several hundred metres away.

Figure 66 – Long and Scenic Tjäktjavagge Valley | Emergency Shelter atop Tjaktja Pass

The landscape had changed dramatically. In the pass, there is almost no life, neither birches nor bush, just tundra grass. Everything looked really rough and rugged with patches of snow lying on the slopes of the surrounding peaks. It was also much busier on the trail today. We passed several people hiking south and a large group leaving Singi, heading for Kebnekaise. It felt like this is where the true tourist section begins, and everything is geared towards them. We even saw a sign today indicating a shop and sauna – the first of its kind – so we know we have definitely reached tourist central.

Day 19: Wild Camp (Tjäktja STF Hut +1km) to Alesjaure STF Hut

Distance:	12.7 km/7.9 miles	Elev. Gain/Loss (m):	+170/-244
Duration:	3.5 hours	Difficulty Level:	easy

This morning, there was ice on the tent and strong winds gusting, so we decided to stay put in our sleeping bags a while longer. Having hiked further along the trail last night, we'd left ourselves with a short 12 kilometres or so to the Alesjaure mountain hut, where we intended camping to enjoy our last sauna on the trail. We'd heard via trail talk that it was arguably the best hut on the Kungsleden by way of shop and sauna, so we had to stop by to see if it was true.

It was a cold, drizzly walk down the valley, but, thankfully, we had the wind on our backs. We felt sorry for the multitude of hikers passing us heading south with red, raw faces, the wind battering them from the front. Every time they passed, they asked how much farther to the next hut and looked very deflated to find out it was still some distance away. We reached the mountain hut by 1:00 PM, so we had an entire afternoon to relax. The reception is very large and the warden very welcoming, producing steaming hot cups of blackcurrant juice to warm us up. We paid the camping fee so we could use the cooking facilities and the sauna during the evening, as we were desperate for a proper wash.

Figure 67 – Waking Up to Frost on the Tent | Modern Reception Area & Shop at Alesjaure

After pitching, we spent the afternoon inside the hut warming up. Wayne lit the fire, and we drank plenty of tea, clock watching waiting for when it was feasible to start cooking dinner. We managed to hold out for 6:00 PM, the mixed sauna time starting at 8:00 PM. After our final sauna on the trail and a good scrub in the adjoining wash room, we finally felt clean after a few days on the trail without proper washing. We were also thoroughly warmed through and, walking back to the tent despite it being windy, it was noticeably a few degrees warmer. We were hopeful for improving weather on our penultimate day on the trail and had our fingers crossed for a dry tent in the morning.

Day 20: Alesjaure STF Hut to Nissonjokk (Campsite inside Abisko National Park)

Distance:	31.2 km/19.4 miles	Elev. Gain/Loss (m):	+199/-321
Duration:	9.5 hours	Difficulty Level:	moderate

It was the best night's sleep we'd had on the entire trail. Huge cumulus clouds were building down the valley in the direction we'd be heading though, but there were also patches of blue sky above, so we were optimistic for a better day. We still hadn't been able to capture any grand valley shots with the incessant rain and complete white-out above. Skierfe remained our best day on the trail in 20 days.

Figure 68 – Hiking through the Verdant Gárdden Valley | Chasing Rainbows

We had breakfast in the hut, then took the tent down. We put on full waterproofs, as the grey clouds rolling in signalled a downpour would be imminent, but in fact it never really came. It was an 8-kilometre walk to the emergency shelter at the end of the lake. We had already decided that we'd take a tea brake inside the hut to give us some respite from the wind, although the southbounders were having a much tougher time with it, as they were walking straight into it. The hut is around a 100-metre detour from the trail along the snow route, but we wanted a good break as we'd planned on a 30-kilometre day!

We were amazed with how many rainbows kept appearing ahead of us, so we stopped and sat on some rocks, admiring the rainbows and the changing intensity of their colours. It was then a steady downhill walk into the Abisko National Park. As wild camping is not permitted in the park and as the mountain hut at Abiskojaure wasn't far enough, we had planned on getting to the national park designated campsite just 4 kilometres out of Abisko. It meant a long day, but it would benefit us the following day with us only having 4 kilometres to go to reach the end of the trail, allowing us plenty of time in Abisko to celebrate!

Figure 69 – Leaving the Bare Mountain Region Behind | Walking on Wooden Tracks

The trail was extremely easy to follow from here. There were lots of new wooden boards that had recently been laid, and what ensued was very steady walking, mostly on flat paths. The boards here have been laid like tracks. We assumed the two sets were for more traffic, so southbounders and northbounders could continue walking at the same time, passing each other without having to give way. But Wayne thought they had been constructed that way for vehicles to get in and out.

We made excellent time, covering around 4.5 kilometres per hour. By 3:30 PM, we'd already hiked 20 kilometres, just 10 kilometres left to go! As the lake finally ends, the trail then follows alongside the river. We were still one step ahead of the rain and marching along the newly constructed boards, when we were startled by a huge reindeer that ran across the trail right in front of us. In fact, there was a large group of them that then all skittered and darted right across the trail. It was the closest we had been to any reindeer, as they usually bolt as soon as they realise a human is in sight.

As we reached the designated campsite, Nissonjokk, it was already a tent village and buzzing with teenagers clearly on a school camp. We walked around looking for a pitch, but as we didn't want to be in the thick of the furore, we picked a more secluded spot at the edge of the area. Wayne said to me "Don't be sad that it's your last camping night!". I wasn't sad about that, just that for our final night on the trail, we wouldn't be camping in an amazing wild camp spot complete with fire pit and awesome view. It didn't take long for us to get into our sleeping bags and drift off after a 30-kilometre day. We awoke twice in the night though and had to look outside the tent and up at the sky just in case the northern lights were appearing above our heads. Unfortunately not, maybe we'll be lucky tomorrow!

Day 21: Nissonjokk (Campsite inside Abisko National Park) to Abisko

Distance:	4.4 km/2.7 miles	Elev. Gain/Loss (m):	+93/-114
Duration:	1.5 hours	Difficulty Level:	easy

We were suddenly woken by big, fat drops landing on the tent around 5:30 AM! That's exactly what we didn't want for our final morning. We had a bag of trail mix left, so we ate that for a quick breakfast, then packed everything away inside the tent. It was a rapid de-camp compared to our usual lengthy two-hour getaway – food and beer waiting at the end of a trail is always a good motivator!

Figure 70 – Fully Prepared in our Wet Weather Gear| Fast-Flowing Abiskojåkka River

We expected the last 100th of the trail to take us around an hour, but it turned out to be a very taxing last few kilometres as the persistent heavy rain through the night had created a trail that was completely saturated. We'd been warned that this section of the trail, above all others, is like a highway. And indeed it was! Freshly groomed and newly kitted-out hikers, expectant for their own Arctic Circle wilderness experience, passed us every few minutes. Some laden with big packs off on a long-distance adventure of their own, some enjoying a weekend jaunt away from the city, all of them smelling of soap and cleanliness, making us ever more conscious of how much we needed to launder our very lived-in clothes!

As we neared the Kungsleden sign signalling our finish, we met an American guy from Maryland who had already been hiking for 10 days in Norway but was now busy getting his gear ready for the off from Abisko to Nikkaluokta. He congratulated us on our achievement. He said it really was an achievement, as he'd never met anyone who'd hiked the entire Kungsleden before. He took our photo and told us where they did a great buffet lunch in town for 100 SEK (£9) p/p. Returning the favour, we told him about some good camp spots we'd seen just outside the national park.

We filmed a little bit of the end, then off we went to the STF Fjällstation for that celebratory beer we'd been hankering after for days! The Fjällstation was extremely busy. People of all ages and nationalities were sprawled out in every nook and cranny around the building, glued to their smartphones, making use of the free Wi-Fi. We, too, wanted a comfy seat and to update social media of our progress! 430+ kilometres later – job done! We savoured the most expensive beer we've ever had, ate an equally expensive but tasty sandwich from the shop, then set off to Abisko Östra, 3 kilometres down the way, to find our hostel for further celebrations and to muse over our Kungsleden adventure. And what an adventure it was!

Figure 71 – Completing the Kungsleden in Abisko

Appendices

A. Elevation Profiles

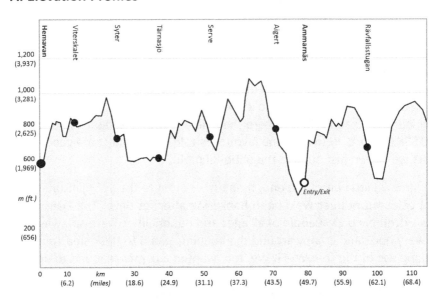

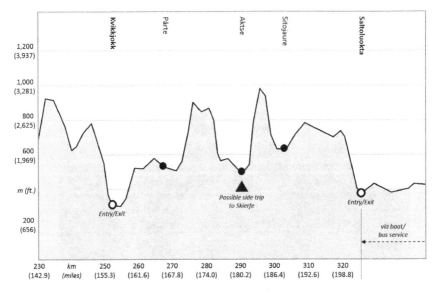

< Appendices >

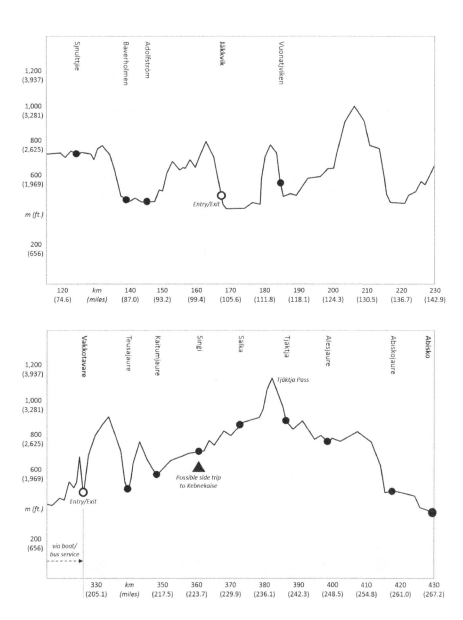

Note: Distances and elevations are based on GPS data recorded by the authors during their trek. Marginal deviations from official numbers are possible due to personal route choices.

B. Trail Overview Map

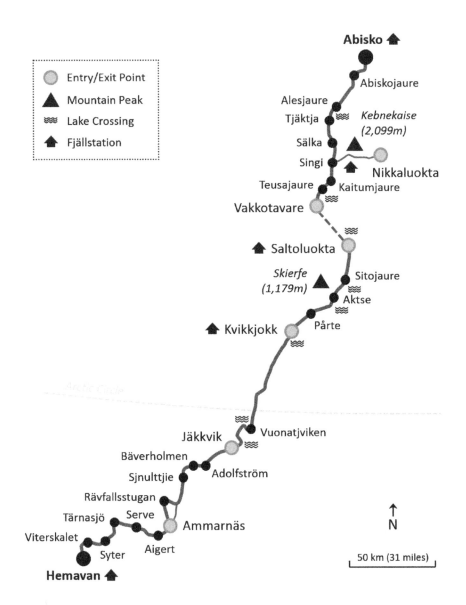

C. Sample Itineraries for Section Hiking

Hemavan to Ammarnäs Section (6 days)

Location	Itinerary	
	day	km (miles)
Hemavan	0	-
Viterskalet	1	11 (6.8)
Syter	2	12 (7.4)
Tärnasjö	3	14 (8.7)
Serve	4	14 (8.7)
Aigert	5	19 (11.8)
Ammarnäs	6	8 (5)
Total	6 days	78 km (48.5 miles)

Ammarnäs to Kvikkjokk Section (8 days)

Location	Itinerary	
	day	km (miles)
Ammarnäs	0	-
Rävfallsstugan*	1	19 (11.8)
Sjnulttjie	2	27 (16.8)
Adolfström	3	21 (13)
Jäkkvik	4	21 (13)
Vuonatjviken	5	18 (11.2)
Tjaurkatan**	6	21 (13)
Goabddabakte**	7	22 (13.7)
Kvikkjokk	8	22 (13.7)
Total	8 days	171 km (106 miles)

*Taking the longer route option out of Ammarnäs.

**Wild camping locations. No huts or cabins.

Kvikkjokk to Saltoluokta Section (4 days)

Location	Itinerary	
	day	km (miles)
Kvikkjokk	0	-
Pårte	1	16 (9.9)
Aktse	2	24 (14.9)
Sitojaure	3	13 (8.1)
Saltoluokta	4	20 (12.4)
Total	4 days	73 km (45.3 miles)

Kvikkjokk to Abisko Section (13 days)

Location	Itinerary	
	day	km (miles)
Kvikkjokk	0	-
Pårte	1	16 (9.9)
Aktse	2	24 (14.9)
Sitojaure	3	13 (8.1)
Saltoluokta	4	20 (12.4)
Vakkotavare*	5	0 (0)
Teusajaure	6	16 (9.9)
Kaitumjaure	7	9 (5.6)
Singi	8	13 (8.1)
Sälka	9	12 (7.4)
Tjäktja	10	12 (7.4)
Alesjaure	11	13 (8.1)
Abiskojaure	12	20 (12.4)
Abisko	13	15 (9.3)
Total	13 days	183 km (114 miles)

* Saltoluokta to Vakkotavare is via the boat/bus service (-> zero hiking kilometres).

Nikkaluokta to Abisko Section (7 days)

Location	Itinerary	
	day	km (miles)
Nikkaluokta	0	-
Kebnekaise	1	19 (11.8)
Singi	2	14 (8.7)
Sälka	3	12 (7.4)
Tjäktja	4	12 (7.4)
Alesjaure	5	13 (8.1)
Abiskojaure	6	20 (12.4)
Abisko	7	15 (9.3)
Total	**7 days**	**105 km (65 miles)**

D. Side Trips

Padjelanta National Park

Padjelanta National Park, or *Badjelánnda* in Sámi language, is Sweden's largest national park and is part of the World Heritage of Laponia. Situated with Sarek in the east and Sulidälbmá in the west, along with the Norwegian border mountains, the park is an alpine landscape of high plains and large lakes. It's no coincidence that Padjelanta means "highland". The terrain is open with soft contours, in contrast to the adjoining Sarek National Park. This gentle form of landscape makes this area's biggest trail, *The Padjelanta Trail*, an excellent alternative for beginners.

In summer, the area is a paradise for alpine flowers. It's also grazing land for reindeer. Around the large lakes, the unique flora attracted botanists as early as the 17th century. The lime-rich bedrock combined with the grazing reindeers have created optimum growing conditions for many unusual species. The few people who lived here used many of the plants as food and herb medicine. Padjelanta also has one of the highest concentrations of ancient remains in the alpine world. If you decide to spend some extra days here, be sure to look out for old reindeer grazing land, settlements, or rocks indicating hearths, which tell you some of the history of Padjelanta.

Sarek National Park

Sarek National Park contains 6 of Sweden's 13 highest mountains and almost 100 glaciers. It is considered a true wilderness area, as it has few signs of human activity, apart from the Lapps' age-old cultivation of the land and the mines around Alkavare and Äpar. The national park is renowned for its large moose and abundance of predators. The migrating reindeer have carved paths into the lush valley floors. In summer, the mountain slopes provide reindeer grazing land for three Sámi communities: Sirges, Jåhkågaska Tjiellde, and Tuorpon.

Hiking in Sarek is demanding, and there are many streams that can be difficult to cross. There are no marked trails or cabins to spend the night in. However, with its long valleys, rivers, glaciers, and distinctive peaks, navigation is not overly difficult when conditions are fine. If you have a reasonable level of backcountry experience, spending a few extra days in Sarek is highly recommended, as it offers a much wilder, off-the-beaten-track experience than the Kungsleden and provides the solitude that is absent in the northern section.

Stora Sjöfallet National Park

Stora Sjöfallet National Park, known as *Stuor Muorkke* in Sámi language, is located 200 kilometres (124 miles) north of the Arctic Circle and forms another piece of the World Heritage of Laponia. The landscape is a mixture of imposing mountain ridges, deep sculpted valleys, high boulder fields, and beautiful pine primeval forests. As in the rest of Laponia, this is an area where you can watch reindeer and moose and, with some luck, even predators like lynx, wolverine, and brown bear. The mountain massif Áhkká is the most characteristic mountain here, also known as the Queen of Lapland.

Laponia

Located in the county of Norrbotten in Lapland, Laponia is the biggest connected natural landscape in Europe. It contains nature that is, to a large extent, still untouched by humans. Designated a UNESCO World Heritage Site in 1996, it is a Sámi cultural landscape with traces of human activity dating back thousands of years.

Vistas STF Mountain Hut

If starting from the north, a popular detour off the Kungsleden is to head southeast from Alesjaure into Vistasvaggi to the Vistas STF mountain hut, which was the first tourist facility in the Kebnekaise area. (It has a small store with supplies.) Vistas presents a lush oasis amongst the brooding mountain range, snow, and glaciers but is considered another backcountry route as there is a path but no markers to follow. There are signs at the relevant crossroads, however, so it's not too difficult to find your way. Stay the night at the hut, then head northwest through Stuor Reidavaggi. Stay (or pass) the small Nallo cabin (no supplies) and continue west to rejoin the Kungsleden at Sälka. Vistasvaggi and Stuor Reidavaggi are considered two of the most beautiful valleys in Swedish Lapland, so it's well worth making the detour if you have both the time and good weather.

Abisko National Park

If you've made your way along the Kungsleden to the northernmost parts of Sweden, Abisko National Park is just one of those must-see places where you can spend a few extra days exploring, as the scenery is truly breathtaking. A combination of snow-capped mountains, valleys, and a rugged, peaceful landscape more than 200 kilometres (124+ miles) north of the Arctic Circle gives Abisko its unique environment that attracts over 40,000 visitors every year. Here, you can trek through boreal forests, hike along fjords, canyons, and waterfalls, go caving, try your hand at fly-fishing, or see Trollsjön, the clearest lake in Sweden in the Kärkevagge valley.

Abisko National Park is also considered the best place in the world for experiencing the Northern Lights. Abisko mountain station is the only hotel in the national park, from which it is a short walk to the chairlift that whisks you up to the Aurora Sky Station. Once at the summit, large balconies provide a perfect vantage point for northern lights watching.

Note: The best time for witnessing the Midnight Sun is between 27th May and 18th July, whereas the Northern Lights usually occur in the winter months November through March!

E. Checklists

These checklists are meant to assist you in your preparations. Depending on your personal preferences, you can add or remove certain items from the lists.

Clothing ( ) indicates optional items

	Hiking socks			Trail hiking boots/shoes
	Underwear			Hat or visor
	Sports bra (women)			Beanie/warm cap
( )	Shorts			Warm neck gaiter
( )	Zip-off hiking pants			Gloves
	Long trousers/pants (hiking or jogging)			Multifunctional scarf for cold/ sun protection
	Long-sleeved T-shirt			Long underwear
	Short-sleeved T-shirt			Sleepwear
	Lightweight rain jacket			Camp shoes/flip-flops
	Lightweight rain pants		( )	Gilet/Waistcoat
	Insulating fleece jacket and/or down jacket		( )	Ankle/leg gaiters for snow/dust

Personal Items (optional)

	Book/e-book reader			Journal
	Notepad, pen			Tripod
	Music player, headphones			Mirror

Gear ( ) indicates optional items

	Backpack		Printouts for all travel arrangements
	Tent		Map and/or map app
	Sleeping bag		Money
	Sleeping pad		Compass
	Stove		Sunglasses
	Fuel		Toilet paper
	Spark striker/lighter		Towel
	Waterproof matches		Headlamp
	Pot		Watch (waterproof)
	Long spoon/utensils		Trekking poles
	Food & snacks		Insect repellent
( )	Water treatment	( )	Eye mask
	Hydration pack or bottles	( )	Sleeping gear (ear plugs, inflatable pillow, etc.)
	Mug (with lid)	( )	Rope
	Pocket knife	( )	Spare water container (collapsible)
	First aid kit	( )	Medication
	Silver survival blanket	( )	Deodorant
	Sunscreen (SPF 30 & up)	( )	Solar charger
	Tooth brush and paste	( )	GPS watch
	Soap (biodegradable)	( )	Moisturiser
	Camera	( )	Lip balm (with SPF)
	Extra batteries & memory card(s)	( )	Trowel
	Passport/Photo ID		

Food List per Day per Person (3 alternatives per meal)

Breakfast	
	Instant oatmeal + dried fruit + almonds
	2 cups muesli/granola + ½ cup dried milk
	Freeze-dried scrambled eggs

Lunch	
	Canned, dried, smoked meat + crackers
	Fish in a pouch with 2 slices of bread
	Peanut butter (individ. cup) and 1.5 oz. crackers

Snacks	
	Nuts and seeds/Dried fruit
	Chocolate bar
	Protein/granola bars

Dinner	
	Freeze-dried instant meal
	1½ cups instant potato, dried veggies + broth
	2 cups pasta, dried tomatoes + herbs

Other Food Items / Condiments

	Sugar
	Coffee (and creamer)
	Powdered milk
	Tea
	Hot chocolate
	Powdered drink mixes

	Salt & pepper
	Spices & herbs
	Hot/soy sauce
	Vitamins & minerals
	Olive oil
	Chocolate, fruity sweets

Resupply

	Extra food rations
	Sunscreen (60g (2oz) per week, min. SPF 30)
	Toilet paper
	Condiments, spices, etc.
	Extra fuel

( )	Celebratory treats
( )	Clean clothing items (T-shirts, underwear, etc.)
( )	Extra batteries
( )	Wet wipes

F. Food Suggestions

Breakfast

- Instant oatmeal (purchase with or add flavours and sugar), porridge, semolina, and polenta with dried fruits
- Self-mixed cereals - with sesame, chia, flax, sunflower, pumpkin and other seeds; raisins and other dried fruit and berries; nuts; coconut flakes; rolled oats, shredded wheat, multi grains, etc.; mixed with dry milk, powdered soy, coconut, or almond milk, and possibly protein powder
- Pumpernickel (dark rye bread), tortilla, pita, or other dense, long-lasting breads
- Almond and peanut butter; tahini (sesame paste); chocolate spread; jam and honey
- Freeze-dried breakfasts (e.g., scrambled egg, hash brown)
- Tea bags, tea pouches (such as ginger granulate), coffee, hot chocolate, sugar

Lunch

- Tinned meat, smoked/dried sausage (e.g., traditional salami), beef and other jerkies
- Tuna and salmon in pouches; tinned fish and mussels in sauces; dried salted fish and shrimp
- Hard-boiled eggs
- Hummus; dried couscous (add boiling water)
- Crackers (wheat, whole grain, quinoa, corn); breads and tortillas
- Peanut butter; squeezy cheese; cheese triangles; pouches of olive oil and herbs; other veggie/vegan spreads
- Aged cheeses (repackaged in breathable material keep well)

Snacks

- Almonds, pistachios, other nuts and seeds (no shells, with/-out flavours, smoked)
- Dried fruits (mango, apricot, banana, date, fig, apple, etc.) and berries; fruit leather
- Power bars and gels; protein, granola, and cereal bars; other candy and snack bars
- Sundried tomatoes, veggie chips, olives in oil
- Dried corn kernels for popcorn in the evening (refine with oil, salt, sugar)
- Chocolate, jelly sweets, hard boiled sweets, fudge (limit these 'empty calories')

Dinner

- Freeze-dried instant meals in pouches – just add boiling water (try different varieties, flavours, and brands prior)
- Pasta with sundried tomatoes, tomato paste, and/or pesto, olive oil and spices, parmesan
- Quinoa, millet, and couscous with herbs and spices with packet tuna (add dried carrots, onion, peas)
- Soup base or stock cubes, add noodles or rice and flakes of mushroom, parsley, tomato, etc.
- Ramen noodles and other instant dishes (e.g., macaroni & cheese, dried mashed potatoes) with instant gravy
- Burritos with rice, packet chicken, beans, cheese, dried bell pepper
- Mixed lentils, beans, and chickpeas with seasoning (keep in mind the cooking times)
- Condiments: salt, pepper, spices, little sachets of mayonnaise, ketchup, hot sauce, soy sauce, olive oil, chili flakes, parmesan
- Herbal tea, instant hot chocolate, hot lemon with honey

G. Contact Information

Hemavan Mountain Station

Fjällstigen 2
92066 Hemavan
+46 (0) 954 30027
info@hemavanfjallstation.se
https://www.swedishtouristassociation.com/facilities/stf-hemavan-mountain-station/

Ammarnäs Wärdshus Hotel & Cabins

Nolsivagen 6
92495 Ammarnäs
+46 (0) 952 602 00
info@fishyourdream.com
http://www.ammarnaswardshus.se/en/

Ammarnäsgården Mountain Hotel & Hostel

Tjulträskvägen 1
92422 Ammarnäs
+46 (0) 952 600 03
fjallhotell@ammarnasgarden.se
http://ammarnasgarden.se/eng/hotel-swedish-lapland/

Getting a Key from Ammarnäs for Rävfallsstugan cabin:

http://www.vindelfjallen.se/news/nyckelsystem-infors-utmed-vindelvaggileden

Getting a Key for Pieljekaisestugan Cabin:

Contact Jäkkvik Life (+46 (0) 961 210 50) or Handelsboden in Adolfström (+46 (0) 961 230 41).

Värdshus – Inn & Cabins (also Camping)

Bäverholmen 1
93893 Laisvall, Arjeplog
+46 (0) 961 23018 or +46 070 28 230 18 (mobile)
baverholmswardshus@hotmail.se
https://www.facebook.com/Baverholm/

Johanssons Fjällstugor/Fjällflygarna – Cabins, Camping & Helicopter

Adolfström 158
93093 Laisvall
+46 (0) 961 230 40
info@fjallflygarna.se
http://www.fjallflygarna.se/

Kyrkans Fjällgård – Hostel

Byavagen 4
93895 Jäkkvik
+46 073 5210369 (mobile)
kyrkans.fjallgard@telia.com
http://www.kyrkansfjallgardjakkvik.com/

Vuonatjviken Holiday Village – Cabins

Vuonatjviken 3
93090 Arjeplog
+46 (0) 961 43031
eva@vuonatjviken.com
http://www.vuonatjviken.com/e_stugby.html

STF Kvikkjokk Fjällstation

Storvägen 19
96202 Kvikkjokk
+46 (0) 971 21022
info@kvikkjokkfjallstation.se
https://www.swedishtouristassociation.com/facilities/stf-kvikkjokk-fjallstation/

STF Saltoluokta Fjällstation

98299 Gällivare
+46 (0) 973 41010
info@saltoluokta.stfturist.se
https://www.swedishtouristassociation.com/facilities/stf-saltoluokta-mountain-station/

STF Kebnekaise Turiststation

98199 Kiruna
+46 10190 23 60
info@kebnekaise.stfturist.se

https://www.swedishtouristassociation.com/facilities/stf-kebnekaise-mountain-station/

STF Abisko Turiststation

98107 Abisko
info@abisko.stfturist.se
https://www.swedishtouristassociation.com/facilities/stf-abisko-mountain-station

Abisko Guesthouse

Kalle Jons väg 5,
98107 Abisko
+46 (0) 70 652 12 64
mail@abiskoguesthouse.com
http://www.abiskoguesthouse.com/en/

Abisko.net – Winterday Hostel/Hostel Haverskog

Tomas & Andreas Haverskog
Lapportsv. 34 A
98107 Abisko
+46 (0) 980 40103
info@abisko.net
http://www.abisko.net/

Swedish Tourist Association – STF Main Office

Fax: + 46 8 678 19 58
info@stfturist.se
https://www.swedishtouristassociation.com/

Naturvårdsverket

Environmental Protection Agency with information on the National Parks.
http://www.naturvardsverket.se/
http://www.swedishepa.se/

Sametinget

Official organisation to represent the Sámi people in their dealings with the State.
www.sametinget.se/english/

H. Links & References

Discover the Swedish Adventure – Swedish Tourist Association

Plan your personalised visit to the trail with basic maps and trail information, detailed STF mountain hut facilities and locations, Fjällstation facilities, and online reservation system, plus latest news.

https://www.swedishtouristassociation.com/

Swedish Meteorological and Hydrological Institute – SMHI

For the latest in-depth and up-to-date weather forecasts for Sweden.

http://www.smhi.se

Swedish EPA – Environment Protection Agency

For the latest information on National Parks and Nature Reserves, guidance and updates to regulations. The Right of Public Access, Protected Areas and Hunting in Sweden. Location maps and contact information. Particularly useful if you intend on visiting points of interest or doing any side trips.

http://www.swedishepa.se/Enjoying-nature/

Calazo Maps

Take a look at this website when deciding what maps you will purchase for your Kungsleden walk.

http://www.calazo.se/

SJ Trains

Look at transport options across Sweden by train. Check routes, timetables, current prices, and make reservations.

http://www.sj.se

Portal for Public Transport in Västerbotten

Check regional transport routes, options, current prices, and make reservations.

http://www.tabussen.nu

Länstrafiken Norrbotten – Long-Distance Bus Services

Northern Sweden – Look at transport options to and from entry and exit points on the Kungsleden by bus. Check routes, timetables, current prices, and make reservations.

http://www.ltnbd.se

Hallingbäck et al. (eds)

If you specifically want to find out more about Swedish flora and fauna, this encyclopaedia covers 262 species in 416 pages.

The text is written in Swedish, but each species has a short English summary with 'Key facts'. Includes many high-quality illustrations, distribution maps, and illustrated identification keys in both Swedish and English, making the book valuable for an international audience.

The National Encyclopaedia of the Swedish Flora and Fauna. Bladmossor: Sköldmossor - Blåmossor / Bryophyta: Buxbaumia - Leucobryum. Nationalnyckeln, 2006.

And, of course, visit:

www.PlanAndGoHiking.com

for more information and pictures.

We look forward to and appreciate your feedback!

I. List of Abbreviations

ASL	Above Sea Level
ATM	Automated Teller Machine/Cash Dispenser
ETD	Estimate of Trail Days
GPS	Global Positioning System
LED	Light Emitting Diode
£	British Pound (currency code: GBP)
PO	Post Office
p/p	per person
SEK	Swedish Krona (Sweden has its own currency as opposed to Euros)
STF	Swedish Tourist Association
UK	United Kingdom
UNESCO	United Nations Educational, Scientific, and Cultural Organization
USA	United States of America
YHA	Youth Hostels Association (England & Wales)

J. Helpful Phrases in Swedish

Bastu	Sauna
Blåbär	Bilberries and wild blueberries
Brandförsvar	Fire protection
Bro	Bridge
Butik	Shop
Fästingar	Tick
Hjälptelefon	Emergency phone
Mygg	Mosquito
Räddningstjänst	Rescue service
Rengärde	Reindeer fence
Resplusbiljett	Special ticket that combines train and long-distance bus travel
Säkerhetsrum	Emergency room
Sieidi	Places of worship
Skicka paket	Send packet
Slask	Waste water
Stugvärd	Warden's hut
Tork	Drying room
Tvatt	Washing
Vatten	Drinking water
Vedbod	Woodshed

About the Authors

English born and bred, Wayne and Danielle have been a couple for 20 years. Their passion for the great outdoors was ignited during their first career break in 2010, when they bought a pair of walking boots for the first time and hiked in various parts of South East Asia, China, New Zealand, and the USA.

Since then, they have completed several thru-hikes at home and around the world, including the Coast to Coast Walk and Pennine Way across England; the 'W' trek in Torres del Paine, Chile; Colca Canyon in Peru; the John Muir Trail in the USA; the West Highland Way in Scotland; and the GR20 across Corsica. They have documented all of their trekking adventures on their 'hiking, travel, and adventure' blog: *www.treksnappy.com*

As Danielle puts pen to paper, writing about their experiences on the trail, Wayne, being the keen photographer of the two, likes to capture the heart and soul of a place on camera, showing the wonders of nature through his images and time-lapse sequences.

While they would love nothing more than to hike full time, currently, Wayne and Danielle are living and working in England, as a means of saving and preparing for their next outdoor adventure!

Special Thanks

We would like to thank our parents, without whom none of our hiking adventures would be possible. Not only have they put a roof over our heads, stored our most treasured possessions, and become foster parents to our two very spoilt cats, but they have also been instrumental to us achieving our goal of completing this journey by becoming our most loyal followers and dedicated 'Support Team'.

You always have faith in us. Words cannot express how grateful we are.

Disclaimer

The information provided in this book is accurate to the best of authors' and publisher's knowledge. However, there is no aspiration, guarantee, or claim to the correctness, completeness, and validity of any information given. Readers should be aware that internet addresses, phone numbers, mailing addresses, as well as prices, services, etc. were believed to be accurate at time of publication, but are subject to change without notice.

References are provided for informational purposes only. Neither authors nor the publisher have control over the content of websites, books, or other third party sources listed in this book and, consequently, do not accept responsibility for any content referred to herein. The mention of products, companies, organizations, or authorities in this book does not imply any affiliation with or endorsement by author(s) or publisher, and vice versa. All product and company names are trademarks™ or registered® trademarks of their respective holders.

This book is not a medical guidebook. The information and advice provided herein are merely intended as reference and explicitly not as a substitute for professional medical advice. Consult a physician to discuss whether or not your health and fitness level are appropriate for the physical activities describe in this book, especially, if you are aware of any pre-existing conditions or issues.

* * *

Made in the USA
Las Vegas, NV
16 June 2024